Still Hot

THE **UNCENSORED** GUIDE
TO DIVORCE, DATING, SEX, SPITE,
AND HAPPILY EVER AFTER

Sue Mittenthal & Linda Reing

RUNNING PRESS

PHILADELPHIA · LONDON

Library of Congress Control Number: 2007938858

ISBN 978-0-7624-3112-0

Book design by Amanda Richmond
Typography: Avenir, Berkeley Book, and Apricot
Author photo © Susan and Alan Gordon

This book may be ordered by mail from the publisher.
Please include $2.50 for postage and handling.
But try your bookstore first!

Running Press Book Publishers
2300 Chestnut Street
Philadelphia, PA 19103-4371

Visit us on the web!
www.runningpress.com

To Nina and Will, with love and gratitude
—S. M.

For Paul and Victoria, each the love of my life, and for my mother, who taught me the power of laughter
—L.R.

LEGAL DISCLAIMER

Contents

Introduction

We'd like to thank our exes for the hilariously predictable behavior that inspired this book. Ditto their new wives—each at least fifteen years their junior, blonde, taut, and taller than them.

How did we get here?

The story began when our husbands imploded. Big time. In textbook fashion.[1] Teetering at middle age, they noticed that half their lives (and hair) had disappeared, and the second half was looking even worse. They scratched their shiny heads and wailed, "Is this all there is?" They dreamed of Ferraris, settled for buzz-cuts, and finally declared, "Do-over."

The babes followed. And pretty soon, the soliloquies from our smitten mates, who ruefully explained, "I have to go where my spirit is leading me."

They went. Up in smoke. Down the path to self-actualization. In quest of eternal youth, and the antidote to male-pattern baldness.

[1] Textbook of Personality Disorders, American Psychiatric Publishing, Inc., 2005

Shell-shocked, we fortified ourselves with Valium, vodka, and voodoo dolls, and hurtled through misadventures of our own. Our odysseys were _____.

A) sob fests

B) dietetic

C) self-medicating

D) sexy

E) a lot like what the Lord did to Job

Correct answer: all of the above

We stumbled through the mire, starting with the girlfriends who slapped us out of our stupor and dragged us shopping for steamy little underthings. Just as bewildering: the so-called sisters who deftly deleted us from their dinner party lists the moment they heard the "D word."

We spent oh-so-lonely Saturday nights playing solitaire on the Internet. Broke out in shingles right before the divorce trial. Discovered the Rabbit and *re*discovered the condom. Sipped lattes with dorks. Handed our hearts to players. And introduced new boyfriends to our kids, whose creep radar was invariably better than our own.

During this topsy-turvy time, we also met for commiseration—every other Thursday in a cafeteria in New York City, over tuna salad, coffee, and a really huge chocolate chip cookie. With, to our surprise, nonstop giggling.

On alternate Thursdays, we ruthlessly mocked our exes, ourselves, and the cast of freaks we dated. We collected stories from other women who had fallen down the same rabbit hole. Pretty soon we were toting legal pads to lunch and logging in tidbits from nearly a hundred fellow travelers. The starter wives of butchers, bakers, and candlestick makers, they were suddenly single and just as dazed as we were. We filled the pads with their mishaps, and the quips, quizzes, and wacky vignettes assumed a life of their own.

Somehow we all muddled through, learned a thing or two, and came out right side up, or close to it. Then we looked back and laughed at the unexpected comedy in it all.

And believe it or not, you will too.

PHASE I:

Your Marriage Is Toast

We're here to give you a heads-up. Is your pin-striped, wing tipped husband of twenty years suddenly swaggering like Mick Jagger and dressing like Ashton Kutcher? He could be in the throes of a midlife tsunami, the kind that churns him around and burps up a mopey, self-centered, walking hair plug.

Once he was Ward Cleaver. Now he's . . . who is he, anyway? He *was* the dad who high-fived Goofy with the kids in front of Cinderella's Castle, and hustled to get Mickey's autograph. He had you racing him over to the emergency room at 3 a.m. for heart palpitations, which turned out to be an anxiety attack. He wore ten-year-old Keds and watched Saturday morning cartoons. If it had been up to him, his IRA would contain all of fourteen dollars. You socked savings away, sure that the two of you would grow old together.

But now that he's on the back nine, he's throwing a hissy fit. One man who's facing fifty revs up a motorcycle, futzes with his comb-over, and calls it a day. Another comes thoroughly unglued, plunging back into adolescence—when a souped-up GTO and a perky cheerleader were all he ever wanted or needed.

If he's talking 400 horsepower and clicking on classmates.com, there's a good chance he's either re-inventing himself or instant messaging someone named Tiffany. Or both.

How to spot an alien

Your husband is morphing, but no single new habit alarms you. You take it with a grain of salt that the new book on his nightstand is The Love Poems of Rumi. *You figure he's just taking a break from* Batman: The Dark Knight Returns. *Next thing you know, he's blubbering to a shrink two, no, three times a week. One day he fantasizes aloud about quitting the accounting game and living on a houseboat in Vancouver.*

What's his damage? There's only one way to find out. Follow him around, keeping a small notepad handy. Jot down changes in his dress, diet, and grooming. Record his idle musings. His new image is a yellow alert. And it's usually just the tip of the iceberg.

His favorite dinner has always been your linguini with sausage and meatballs, and he's a charter member of the Clean Plate Club. That's why he wears a size 46 waist. Lately he volunteers to stir-fry tofu and bok choy. At the same time, you catch him looking in the mirror regularly while sucking in his gut.

Black turtlenecks and a leather bomber jacket are his new signature look. He donated his plaid flannel shirts to the Salvation Army, as well as those pants with the Magic Stretch waistbands.

You find men's moisturizer in the medicine cabinet. Next to his Crest whitening strips. And his Just for Men hair dye kit.

He bought a selection of Calvin Klein black and gray boxer briefs, and threw away his tighty-whiteys with the skid marks.

He's suddenly into manscaping. He shaves his back and you wonder how he can reach around to all those hard-to-get-to places.

You notice a tiny tattoo on his shoulder: a charging stallion.

He grows a soul patch and wears a small silver hoop earring. *Très* hip.

You always liked the subtle scent of the Armani cologne you bought him. Now he enters the room in a cloud of patchouli oil.

He's Googled the top plastic surgeons in your area and picked up a new habit: gazing into the rearview mirror while pulling up the skin around his eyes.

He wants to trade in the Chevy Suburban, and is deciding between a red Porsche and a Harley Fat Boy.

He's taking up the electric guitar. Every night he spends hours in the basement, figuring out the solo from "Stairway to Heaven."

His new group of friends includes thirty-year-old performance artists with spiked hair. They have affectionately dubbed him "Meal Ticket."

He greets you, the kids, and his mother the same way: "Yo, dude."

He used to read the *Wall Street Journal*; now he studies the *I Ching*.

He could never even bend over to pick up his underwear from the floor. Yet miraculously he's spending hours in the lotus position.

His car radio is no longer set to NPR. These days he walks around wired to an iPod, and he's suddenly well-versed in gangsta rap.

He expresses a profound desire to own a boat, even though he can barely swim and suffers from motion sickness every time he takes a ferry.

Although an actuary for an insurance company, he

refers to himself as "an artist with a day job."

You find a bag of weed in his shaving kit.

Are you still with us? Of course you are. Sorry, baby.

Your husband, the chick magnet

Now that he's got his cool new image down, he's looking to show somebody how hot he is. And it's not you. More likely, it's a junior associate named Ashley or Morgan. You'll find evidence everywhere, from the cuddling-koalas charm you pull out of his suit pocket (inscribed "XOXO, Ash"), to the long blond hairs on the passenger seat of his car. Which are not from your golden retriever. Because they have dark roots— under your magnifying glass.

Raise the threat level to Code Orange.

For twenty years he's left the bill paying to you. Now he grabs the statements for his cell phone, turnpike tolls, and MasterCard the instant they arrive. Later, while preparing your taxes, you see credit card charges for 1-800-FLOWERS, La Perfumerie, and Godiva chocolates. Not to mention match.com and the Hair Club for Men.

He used to spend his weekends playing miniature golf on the computer and adjusting the float ball in the toilet tank. Now he bolts for the office on Saturday mornings because he and his assistant, Samantha, "get so much more accomplished."

Every holiday you hoped for a new watch, but instead he showered you with tire gauges and dehumidifiers. Suddenly a Rolex appears. His guilt is your new best friend.

When he phones to say he'll be home late, his excuses are elaborately detailed: he had to drive his friend to the emergency room, but there was a bottleneck on the bridge, due to an overturned beer truck, followed by a steam pipe explosion and a water main break. Oh yeah, and by the way, he somehow left his socks at the office.

A rep from "Money Mutual" calls to speak to your husband, and you take a message. "Just tell him his checking is overdrawn again," she says. Odd. All of your accounts are joint and at Bank of America. Or so you thought.

He stammers over your first name to avoid confusing you with someone else. You've become "Hon."

Although he's a postal employee, his work now calls for multiple business trips and new weekend hours.

Sex with you is no longer even a blip on his radar screen. His eyes will remain glued to The History Channel even if you strut around naked in fetish heels.

You stop by the pharmacy to pick up his Lipitor. You open the bag and find a six-month refill of Viagra, which you know he hasn't used with you—unless, despite the hype, it doesn't work.

We think you know what comes next.

Keyword: cheating

Be alert to suspicious activity surrounding your husband's high-tech gizmos. These are a dead giveaway. Especially if you know how to hack.

- *Has his BlackBerry turned into a CrackBerry addiction?*
- *Is he up at two in the morning, IM'ing "the office"?*
- *Did he schlep a laptop on your family trip to the Grand Canyon?*
- *And make nine secretive Airphone calls from the plane?*
- *As if he's the Secretary of State?*
- *On Air Force One?*
- *When he's really a Rite Aid pharmacist in coach?*

This is credible intelligence. Elevate the homeland security risk to SEVERE, and prepare for evacuation—his.

Out of nowhere, his cell phone reception has permanently deteriorated—but only at home. He now needs to leave the house in order to get a signal. He does this furtively and often.

You turn on the computer and notice his new screen name: "HotRod287."

Suddenly he has a weak bladder. Every time you go out to dinner, he uses the facilities at least three times. You catch him tucking away his BlackBerry as he emerges from the men's room.

Remember how you used to sit with your legs slung across his lap while you watched TV? Now his cell phone occupies your spot. Plus he leaves the room during the last four minutes of the Super Bowl because he just got a text message.

Does Liz's experience sound familiar? Before her husband went on a business trip, she asked how to reach him at his hotel. "I'll be in suite 1277, but just call my cell," he replied. "I turn off the room phone because I get wrong numbers all night long." *Uh-huh.* Liz didn't have to be Nancy Drew to figure out the following:

- He wasn't staying at that hotel.
- In fact, there wasn't a room 1277 at that hotel.
- Because there were only seven floors in that hotel.
- He wasn't even in the city where the hotel was located.
- His business associates weren't coming along.
- He didn't want to be disturbed.
- Particularly by Liz.

Every time you walk by, he immediately shuts down the computer.

When he goes to take a shower, he stashes his Black Berry in the pocket of his robe and locks the bathroom-door. It's a good fifteen minutes before he turns on the water.

While your family vacations at a lakeside cottage, he's pacing the dock. Every other day, he drives forty miles to an Internet café, claiming that "they have the only authentic espresso in the area."

You find him crunched in the closet, whispering on his cell phone while pretending to select a tie.

When you go online to Google a restaurant, you notice that the most recently visited website on the computer is russianladies.com.

And that he put a personal password on his Word documents. After you guess it in thirty seconds, you find drafts of letters to "Svetlana, my *zaichik*[2]."

Rifling through the filing cabinet, you spot a new folder marked "Travel." Inside, you find MapQuest directions from Minsk to Kiev.

Oh, sweetie. The worst is yet to come.

[2] Bunny rabbit

"If I stay with you,
I'll just become an old man"

Early one morning you check HotRod287's inbox and receive an IM: "Love you big guy. Tiff."

"Who's Tiff?" you ask him over breakfast.

"Oh, just a pen pal," he says lightly. But then he gives it up without much prodding: yes, yes, he's madly in love. It's passionate, it's spontaneous, it's all about music and poetry. He wants to start his adult life over again. Without you.

Or perhaps your husband refuses to fess up. Instead he whines that he's unhappy and needs some space. In fact, he's loaded a backpack and his lease begins on Tuesday. His new place is so cool—it's kinda like the treehouse he had when he was nine.

You're ready to hammer him over the head with a cast-iron skillet. Resist this urge, if humanly possible. But more important, don't quiz him about what went wrong. Do you really need to hear that you don't jog fast enough? That's what you'll get. He'll trot out a litany of trumped-up charges, from the petty to the absurd:

"You always put that green mud on your face at night."
"You made me take off my shoes after you washed the kitchen floor."

"You didn't let me floss in bed."

"You refused to wear a French maid's uniform for me."

"You never wanted to discuss the Spanish Civil War."

"You controlled the thermostat."

"You hid the salt shaker."

"You never liked my mother."

"You knew I wanted a two-seater, but we got a minivan."

"You wouldn't hang my Derek Jeter photo in the living room."

"You rained on my parade."

"I've been miserable since the honeymoon"

Don't believe this revisionism. Look through family albums and count picture after picture of his beaming mug. Re-read the cards he gave you on Valentine's Day. Now go ahead and light the bonfire.

You're no more responsible for his wretched state than you are for his receding hairline. His about-face is a direct result of his fear of death and decrepitude, especially if three or more of these statements are true:

- He recently attended a funeral.
- His life insurance application was denied.
- His lawyer suggested estate planning.
- Which gave him irritable bowel syndrome.

- His blood pressure is a little high.
- His cholesterol is on the rise.
- Everything else is sagging.
- His beer belly has turned into a full keg.
- The tailor had to let out his seams.
- He has more hair in his ears than on his head.
- He can't move without the Bengay after a workout.
- The trainer at the gym calls him "sir."
- The young guys at the office never invite him to happy hour.
- Your daughter laughs much louder at her boyfriend's jokes than at his.

It's a lot to take in. We know. We're with you. Soon you'll be glad he's not.

LET'S REVIEW:
WHAT YOU NOW KNOW

✓ Your chubby hubby has removed the piles of clothing from his old exercise bike.

✓ He willingly eats bean curd.

✓ He religiously applies hair volumizer.

✓ A Mustang convertible with flame decals is sitting in the driveway.

✓ With "Born to Run" blasting from the stereo.

✓ And in the glove compartment, a receipt from the Ritz-Carlton. Room service for two.

✓ He now has the bank statements mailed directly to his office.

✓ His assistant selected your last anniversary gift—a fountain pen.

✓ You can get surveillance software for the family PC for as little as $49.

✓ Tip: his secret password is your home address. How clever.

✓ Why he has the complete Berlitz course on conversational Russian.

✓ He's on Prozac and repeats his new mantra: "We're all going to die someday."

✓ It's all over when he acts like a lovesick teenager.

✓ And calls you a wet blanket.

✓ He packed up the Derek Jeter photo.

PHASE II:

You Gotta Go to the Girls

The world as you know it has come to an end. Your husband's dresser drawers are empty, your marriage is roadkill, and you're having trouble putting one foot in front of the other.

Just getting up and facing the day fills you with dread. Once you're out, every woman you see is wearing a wedding band. She may weigh 350 pounds; she may shuffle behind a walker; she may even have a mustache. Regardless, she has a husband, and you don't.

When evening comes around, you head for your bedroom with a carafe of red wine (for the antioxidants, of course). Make that a magnum on weekends. You never thought you'd actually wish for Monday morning.

On the bright side, your highly sensitive Chihuahua, who piddled his anxiety all over your kitchen floor for the past year, became housebroken again the day your husband left.

Now that he's gone, you'll start to perk up too.

But don't lie in bed analyzing how you "lost" him. Was it your warning that he'd be throwing up constantly on that houseboat in Vancouver? Your insistence that he slather suncreen on his head before zipping off in his Miata? Maybe you *should* have been well-versed on the Spanish Civil War. Stop it. Over thinking is your enemy.

And honey, what you really need now is friends.

Give this girl an "A"

Your married girlfriends will straighten you out of the fetal position. They'll carry you into the lawyer's office and deliver you to a shrink. And they'll pick up your kids from band practice when you're too sedated to drive.

But you'll also need single women friends. Here's why:

1) You'll have more fun sobbing over The Way We Were *if you share the popcorn and Kleenex.*
2) Married people go out with other couples on Friday and Saturday nights. Remember?
3) Your divorced girlfriends will offer unending comfort as they confirm that all ex-husbands are hounds.

Married or single, a friend like this ranks at the top of the class:

You confide to her all the messy details of your breakup. Over time, you realize that she never leaked a word about your husband's affair with **Traci, Spiritual Consultant & Tarot Card Reader (by appointment only)**.

The minute your friend hears that your husband has moved out, she whisks you off to Linens 'n Things for fresh bedding. You're relieved to finally dump those hideous flannel sheets that he had since college. You don't care what he said—they certainly never seemed very "lucky" to you.

She shepherds you to Victoria's Secret, and doesn't snort or snicker when you try on the rhinestone-studded g-string and matching bra.

She treats the death of your marriage like a *shivah* call, cooking chicken soup with matzo balls and packing it into Tupperware so your children and dog don't starve.

She has a job, husband, three kids, and a hamster, but still takes time to drive you home from the colonoscopy she forced you to stop avoiding.

She and her husband attend a business dinner and are

seated with your ex and his arm candy. The next day your pal calls you at the crack of dawn, eager to report that after one white wine spritzer, the girlfriend got weepy and described her botched breast augmentation to the whole table—which included your husband's boss and his wife.

She throws you a fiftieth birthday party featuring a male belly dancer who gives you a foot massage and a French pedicure.

Determined to get you out there, she insists that you frequent temples of testosterone, and rushes you to the nearest NASCAR racetrack.

She invites you to her dinner parties even though you're the only single person there, and refuses to serve the key lime pie until her other guests come up with at least one good man for you to date. They have to collect your phone number before they can get their coats back.

One evening while you're frying meatballs, she calls and barrages you with bizarre questions: "Would you rather go four-wheeling through the woods or have drinks on a veranda at sunset? What's your rising sign? If you could be any kind of cheese, which would you be?" The next day she proudly presents your new Internet dating profile: "Fun, Fit, and Cooks, too."

She sends a heartfelt condolence card to her recently

widowed male neighbor—with a P.S. offering your name, number, and photograph.

She drags you to a singles bar and invites any guy who looks like a pinup from the FDNY Firefighters Calendar to join in a toast to your divorce. Meanwhile, you're still working on hiring a lawyer.

Three Cosmopolitans later, she has a brainstorm. The two of you weave your way to your husband's girl-friend's house, where you proceed to knock over all of her planters and pee in her azaleas.

After running into your husband at the drugstore, she reports back that he was buying Rogaine by the gallon. With a large side order of Preparation H.

What would you possibly do without her? You'd need at least double the Valium, for sure.

Third wheel

Being the odd girl out can land you in some awkward situations, and you need to be prepared. For instance, your best friend and her husband invite you out to dinner. You pull out your wallet when the check comes, but he insists on paying. What do you do?

A) Reach over and grab the bill out of his hand. Whip out your calculator and hand him $23.97, which is your share, including tax and tip.
B) Say thanks, go out with them again, and next time order only a roll and water.
C) Treat them to a night on the town within your budget. Taco Bell.
D) Wow them with your home cooking.

OVEN-BARBECUED CHICKEN

1 cup ketchup

1 cup salsa

½ cup honey

1 tablespoon
   vegetable oil

2 tablespoons
   Dijon mustard

2 teaspoons
   chili powder

1 teaspoon
   ground cumin

3 pounds
   skinless
   chicken thighs

1 tablespoon
   cornstarch

Preheat oven to 400°F.

Whisk together first seven ingredients. Generously coat a 13 x 9 baking dish with nonstick spray. Place chicken in pan and cover with sauce, coating on both sides.

Bake uncovered for 45 minutes. Arrange thighs on serving platter and keep warm. Pour sauce into saucepan.

In small bowl, mix cornstarch with 1 tablespoon water till smooth. Add to sauce and cook till it thickens, stirring constantly. Pour extra sauce over chicken or serve on the side for dipping.

How easy was that?

Correct answer: D) for a total of $6.37. If your guests have any manners at all, they'll bring the wine.

Give this girl an "F"

Most of your friends will rally in your hour of need. Unfortunately, some may run for their lives, as if you're spewing the Ebola virus. Then there's the occasional no-goodnik whose "I'm there for you" sounds suspiciously like this:

She offers her shoulder and you pour your heart out. Three days later, at the gynecologist's office, the receptionist pulls you aside and whispers, "*Oh my gawd*! I hear your husband dumped you for a tarot card reader."

She specializes in *schadenfreude*.[3] Once she learns that your marriage is kaput, nothing gives her more pleasure than blocking your cart at the supermarket and bellowing, "How humiliating! My heart bleeds for you."

She urges you to do whatever it takes to get him back. Before you know it, she's enrolled you in a pole-dancing class.

"Are you sure he was getting enough?" the witch asks. "Come over and I'll teach you. Bring two bananas."

She keeps "forgetting" to introduce you to her next-door neighbor, the widowed investment banker who, in his spare time, studies massage therapy and Cordon Bleu cooking.

The only good byproduct of your grief and aggravation

[3] Lives to savor the misery of others

is that you've gone from a size 12 to a 6 on the Divorce Diet. Determined to get you back up to 150 pounds, she insists that you look haggard and need some Krispy Kremes.

She no longer invites you to her parties, ever since her sister's husband got plastered at the last one, leered at you, and announced repeatedly, "Doesn't she look hot?"

She lives out her fantasies through you, convincing you to buy a see-through shirt and wear it when you pick up your car from the twenty-five-year-old mechanic she referred you to.

Recently divorced herself, she traps you into sharing all the dirty details of your marital demise. "Do tell," she demands. You spill your sordid saga, then ask for hers. "I can't," she demurs. "I promised myself privacy."

She implores you not to reconcile with "that scumbag." Never ever. Three months later she asks, "Would you mind if I gave him a call?"

She bumps into your ex and his new squeeze, wearing matching parrot hats and coconut bras, at a Jimmy Buffet concert. You ask her a thousand questions: "Is she thinner than me? Is she older than my kids? How did she look in a grass skirt?" Her only answer: "Oh, please. Grow up." *Biatch*.

She runs into your husband at the gym and reports, "He's gotten really buff."

Divorce her. You're already going through one—this'll be cake.

Watch your back

As bad as those frienemies can be, sometimes it turns out you've been duped by a double agent. Ditch these Benedict Arnolds for aiding and abetting your husband's trysts:

- The couple who let him nest in their apartment with his girlfriend while he was married to you.
- And left a bottle of champagne for them in the fridge.
- Or covered for him, like when you were sixteen and told your girlfriend's mom that she was sleeping at your house—when she was really in the back seat of her boyfriend's '68 Cutlass Supreme.
- Anyone who knew of his affair a year or more before you did.
- Your "best buds," who invited the lovebirds over to dinner so they wouldn't be seen cooing at each other in a restaurant.
- Married pals of yours who now double-date with them,

and describe her as "young, but sweet."
- And can't wait to drop the bomb: "They're working on having a baby."
- Wishy-washy chums who think they're like Switzerland and can remain neutral forever. Real friends would be willing to trash him regularly and poison his girlfriend's food slowly.

These people are traitors. They should rot in Guantánamo Bay. Short of that, cross them off your Christmas card list.

It's the ME show

Sure you need to vent, and your faithful friends are willing to listen. For a while. However, you can easily become so self-absorbed that you forget to wish your sister a happy birthday while you stew about who your husband was really with on that "corporate" retreat in Cancun. And why his frequent flyer account is empty. You're in danger of driving away friends and family if any of the following has occurred:

Your outgoing cell phone calls outnumber your incoming calls by 400 percent.

Everyone mysteriously has to hang up while you're in mid-sentence.

Including telemarketers.

Friends urge you to get out more and cultivate a hobby. They insist that keeping up a journal for your therapy sessions doesn't count.

Your mother won't take your call because *Judge Judy* is on.

You're not listening while your sister proudly announces her Weight Watchers Lifetime Achievement Award. That's because you're counting the seconds until you can describe your shrink's latest insights into *you*.

You use e-mail the way you used a personal diary when you were thirteen. You bombard your friends with more than they want to know. The only replies you receive are forwarded jokes and recipe chain letters.

Your book club disbands abruptly. Two weeks later, they start a new one without you.

You hear your best friend vacuuming on the other end of the line while you obsess about who's cuter—the dog groomer or the UPS guy.

Your therapist gets up and hangs curtains while you're free-associating.

You tell your neighbor about yet another fascinating dream. She interrupts and asks, "Is this the one where your husband removed the brakes from your car? Or when you knocked him off a ladder and he broke his back?"

It was the one about the brakes missing.

Frankly, you're starting to bore yourself.

She's not *your* mother, amen

You've been good friends with your mother-in-law for decades, so when she first learns that her son wants to start a new life, she threatens to write him out of her will. Here's what Beth's mother-in-law said to her:

- *"He is a cancer. Cut him out of your life immediately."*
- *"How could he do this to you, the kids, and the dog?"*
- *"WE have to get a lawyer."*
- *"Make sure WE get the house."*
- *"That dumpy little bitch."*

Although your mother-in-law loves you, these lines of allegiance will inevitably break down. After all, the sun rises and sets with her boy. Plus she needs someone to drive her to her mah-jongg game. Here are some clues that she won't be sitting on your side of the table at the deposition:

She stops inviting you to her Saturday morning yoga class. Furniture shopping for her son's bachelor pad is her new path to inner peace.

When your husband comes back into your house to claim his possessions, she sends him with a typewritten list, which includes the cocktail-olive picks, KitchenAid mixer, and Lladro figurines—none of which he ever knew existed.

Even though he left you twelve days after your third child was born—for Krystal, a stripper at a go-go bar in New Jersey—his mother makes a point of telling everyone, "There are two sides to every story."

She spreads the word that you're "more frigid than a meat locker."

A few months later, she meets his new girlfriend. "That dumpy little bitch" is now "such a darling girl."

Your son goes off to college right after the breakup, and she attributes his D average to "the poor teaching methods at that university." Never mind that Dad plans to have a new baby.

A year later, when you finally scrounge up a date, she admonishes, "What kind of example are you setting for the children?"

She has a strange new interest in tarot cards and tofu.

As much as all this makes you want to smash the Faberge egg she gave you, take the high road. Sell that puppy back to her favorite antiques shop.

LET'S REVIEW:
WHAT YOU NOW KNOW

✓ Your girlfriends are either Bettys or Veronicas.

✓ Any pal worth her salt will ransack your drawers and throw away your white cotton Granny panties.

✓ And insist that you buy a sheer thong in siren red.

✓ With *You Wish* spelled out across the front.

✓ So the least you could do is ask how her root canal went.

✓ How to throw a dinner party for ten bucks.

✓ What *schadenfreude* means. And why it's safer to order your groceries online.

✓ You should say "Thanks but no thanks" to the two-faced chum bearing Krispy Kremes.

✓ Or bananas.

✓ Your couple friends can choose custody of you or your husband, not both.

✓ His girlfriend's implant is migrating.

✓ Why her azaleas are dead.

✓ The line between "mother" and "mother-in-law" is double-yellow.

✓ A Faberge egg can buy you quite the stockpile of sedatives.

✓ Life goes on, even without the Lladro kissing swans.

PHASE III:
Divorce Jihad

*P*repare yourself for new levels of nausea. Until now, your most gagifying memories go something like this:

- Your son borrowed Petey, the second-grade class rodent. On the way home, Petey ran amok in the car and scrambled all over your sandaled feet and under the brake. You squashed him flat at the next stop sign.
- You strolled by a fish store on a hot July morning, inhaling the scent of sun-warmed salmon during the third month of your pregnancy.
- You asked your neighbor for her special macaroni and cheese recipe, which you and the kids enjoyed so much. She proudly disclosed her secret ingredient—a half cup of her own personal breast milk.

These are a picnic compared to what's in store. Get ready for the ultimate upchuck: divorce. Load your purse with barf bags and step into a free fall. Grab on to your rip cord—but hold on to that pocketbook too, unless your husband is offering the moon. He won't, because he has a lawyer. And a girlfriend. And the morals of a cockroach.

So hang tough. When he demands everything except the dog, don't throw up your hands and sigh, "Oh well, at least I got the dog—and the pooper-scooper too."

Hired killer

Your husband's e-mails are coming fast and furious, exploding with aggressive CAPITAL LETTERS AND EXCLAMATION POINTS!!!! You need protection, and it doesn't come cheap. Whatever the cost, sign up the best attorney in town, even if you have to skip the salon and stop by Wal-Mart for a box of root touch-up. Here's the lowdown on lawyer-shopping:

Brotherhood can be powerful. Cindy's soon-to-be-ex had just lost his job. "I feel sorry for him," her attorney said in male solidarity. Never mind that *she* wouldn't be able to collect alimony. In the settlement, Cindy got to keep her tennis racquet.

Steer clear of the pit bull attorney who sinks her teeth

into her opponent's leg and locks her jaw. Do you really need to make your ex so angry that he demands half the value of the three pieces of jewelry he bought you over the course of your twenty-year marriage?

You'll instinctively choose a lawyer who reflects your personality. So if you never let an angry word roll off your tongue, you'll latch onto a wimp. This is a scientific fact.[4]

Amy's idea of the perfect Friday night is watching *Terms of Endearment* for the sixteenth time with a roll of cookie dough. Her husband's favorite movie is *Rambo,* accompanied by a bag of beef jerky.

True to form, Amy selected an attorney who'd been divorced herself and was sisterly and sympathetic. At a heated point during the trial, her $300-an-hour "advocate" fled to the ladies room, where Amy found her weeping at the sink. Still a billable hour, by the way.

Amy provided an arm to lean on as they returned to the courtroom, only to be eaten alive by the barracuda that her bloodthirsty husband had wisely hired.[5]

If you were raised to be a good girl, you'll need deprogramming. We recommend the following regimen, developed by an alpha male think tank.

---

[4] "Passive women pick gutless divorce lawyers, despite abundant SOBs, Annals of the Matrimonial Bar, January 2007, volume 14"

[5] Two months later, Amy's attorney quit the law altogether. She now sells beaded jewelry on the side of a highway in New Mexico.

- Quit meditating. Learn to punch your fist through a wall.
- Go off your tranquilizers. Temporarily.
- And throw away the Midol.
- Play paintball. Better yet, attend bullfights weekly.
- Ditch your Enya CDs. Stock up on a death metal collection.[6]
- No more pink chick drinks. Switch to bourbon.
- Take up sumo wrestling. Or gang warfare. Pack some heat.
- Weave in and out of traffic and cut off other drivers.
- Then when you get hopelessly lost, refuse to ask anyone for directions.

Okay, now you're a beast. So get out there and hire a terminator. That'll be the lawyer your husband refers to as **DARTH VADER, ESQ**.

Keep in mind that your attorney is not your therapist. Don't call to vent about how pathologically cheap your husband is, or engage her in a critique of his twisted psyche. Every time you feel like unloading on her, think: *kaching kaching*. There goes a cashmere sweater.

And remember, you won't get reimbursed under your mental health benefits. Even worse, lawyers can't prescribe meds.

---

[6] A subgenre of heavy metal music—more brutal, significantly less pleasant

On that subject: sign up for the best prescription drug plan your company offers.

Your lawyer doesn't want to know about the cash you stashed in your best friend's safe deposit box. Keep your mouth shut, and quietly treat yourself to a $200 bra.

Although your divorce attorney is the only man who hangs on your every word, don't fall in love with him. Melanie had an affair with hers, and was shocked to find charges on her final bill for hours they'd spent together in a hotel room. Not to mention the phone calls they made to arrange dates.

As for mediation, as far as we know it's only been successful for three people in the world. We haven't met them yet.

And they're probably really annoying.

CHOOSE YOUR WEAPON

Don't jump to hire the first divorce lawyer you meet, just because she agrees that your husband should be castrated and her assistant calms you with a cup of chamomile tea. The more attorneys you interview, the wiser the choice you'll make. Use our legal aid chart to sort out their styles.

Exhibit A	*Verdict*
Your husband recommends him because "he's fair."	"Fair" = husband maintains cool, high-roller lifestyle. Never mind that *you're* the client.
She promises to get you the same deal as Ivana Trump.	Um, sure. As if you're fortunate enough to be divorcing the Donald.
He'll let you call all the shots.	So why are you paying him $300 an hour?
She badmouths her adversaries.	She'll make enemies on your dime.
He shoots the breeze about his kids, Harvard's admissions standards nowadays, and the price of a gallon of unleaded regular.	You could chat for free with your manicurist, and even pick up a few Korean phrases.
She'll be available to you 24/7.	She has no other clients.
He charges top dollar but: —speaks directly and to the point. —would rather not squander your children's inheritance on litigation. —can dazzle the judge if he has to. —is described by other lawyers as "painful to deal with." —has a sizable male clientele. (Think potential fix-up dates.)	**Sign the retainer.**

No more Mr. Nice Guy

Your husband insists that he will always take care of you and the kids, no matter what. However, when you learn that your E-ZPass has just been canceled—at the tollbooth with a mile of cars honking behind you—you'll realize that his largesse no longer extends to you.

After he walks out on you and the kids, his brain will undergo a lobotomy. All guilt-and-shame gray matter will be sliced out, to be replaced by a mass of seething rage. That way, he won't have to give you any money. Convenient.

Case in point: When he left, his e-mails read, *"You've been a wonderful wife and mother. I'm sorry if I hurt you."* Within a few months, they'll say, *"So shovel the driveway yourself if the kid next door wants fifty bucks."*

If you tell him the children need a math tutor, the dog has fleas, and the boiler is blasting carbon monoxide, you'll find yourself hollering into a black hole. Let your attorney muscle him, and save your breath for a cardio-PUNCH workout.

You're making ends meet by setting ketchup bottles upside down. Meanwhile, your husband plays Sugar Daddy to the kids. Your son parties nightly on beer and weed at college—because Dad gives him an allowance that exceeds the gross national product of Sri Lanka.

Your husband may resort to guerilla warfare. "This is between you and me," he says. "No lawyers. Let's make a deal." Beware. His notion of an equitable split: he gets the stock portfolio; you walk away with everything in the linen closet.

Things can go downhill from there. Larry demanded that Bonnie get the monogrammed wedding silver appraised and buy half of it back from him. Cheap-ass.

Your husband undoubtedly squandered wads of your money on his girlfriend. Diane's ex lavished $100,000 from joint savings on goodies for Amber, a topless dancer, including a chinchilla-trimmed satin robe, Manolo Blahnik stilettos, laser hair-removal treatments, and an amethyst bellybutton ring (she's an Aquarius).

Not to mention twenty cases of French champagne for romantic bubbly baths. Diane was entitled to half that $100K back. (She passed on her share of the used Moët & Chandon.) But her ex blamed his extravagant spree on a cocaine habit and off-track betting. Hoping for leniency, he even forged attendance certificates from Gamblers' Anonymous and the Betty Ford Clinic.

Franny hired a forensic accountant after she noticed a missing chunk of marital assets and her husband's new taste for lemongrass. The accountant's computations: ($200,000 withdrawn from savings + 12 Southeast Asian business trips per year) x (4 Siam Grill takeout meals/week) = 1 additional family in Bangkok. *Kwaam bpra-laat jai*!!![7]

Lucy's husband played the glaucoma card. He shuffled into court with dark, wraparound sunglasses and a cane. A week after the trial, he got his pilot's license.

Don't be surprised if your husband's income takes a nosedive just before your divorce. Accountants call this RAIDS.[8] We call it FRAUD. To wit:

- The day before he filed for divorce, Anne's husband came home from work and waved a pink slip in her face. "Why did he get fired?" she wailed. "He always bragged that he could do his job with one hand tied behind his back." His boss later explained: "From 9 to 5 he did nothing but play Minesweeper on his computer. But every day he managed to drag himself out for sushi and a martini on his expense account."

- Stephanie's husband was a dentist who brightened enough smiles to keep up an apartment in the city and a house in the country. After he moved out, his declared income plummeted to $16,000 a year. That equals four crowns, one bridge, and an impacted wisdom tooth.

[7] "Surprise!!!"
[8] Recently Acquired Income Deficiency Syndrome

• Sometimes RAIDS is part of a long-term plan. Two years before he walked out, Sally's husband quit his proctology practice because he was inspired to write "the next *Harry Potter* series." He produced his opus during litigation: a lined pad titled "Hey, Harry!" followed by eight pages of chicken scrawl and doodles.

Crazy like a fox. His new literary life saved him thousands in support. Get the picture? This is a street fight over a pot of gold. He doesn't care if you waste away on Meow Mix. And they talk about a woman scorned.

Bachelor in paradise?

Your husband is convinced that your attorney was put on this planet for the sole purpose of thwarting *him*. He shoots you a snarky e-mail: *"What's with your lawyer's big butt? Maybe she should have two chairs at the settlement meeting—one for each cheek."*

His venom level is really about the enormous gap he just discovered between his freewheeling, single-dude fantasies and the letdown of his real life.

Wet dream:

As soon as he gets rid of you and hooks up with the prom queen, he'll be eighteen again, lush mane of hair streaming in the wind as he floors his Corvette down an endless stretch of desert highway. Aerosmith booms from the stereo as he pumps his fist in the air.

Cold shower:

It's Thanksgiving Day. He's waiting for the rinse cycle in the laundromat and wolfing down a pressed-turkey sandwich (low sodium).

- His doctor warned him to lose weight.
- The babe demanded that he double the Viagra.
- His accountant said he can only afford a Saturn. If it's pre-owned.
- The barber couldn't camouflage his bald spot. The only solution: surgical scalp reduction.
- The dryer ate his sock.

In his mind, this is all your lawyer's fault.
Obviously.

Call his bluff

View your legal negotiations as a high-stakes poker game: never show your hand, and play like you're holding a royal flush. Let your well-paid, cold-blooded attorney do the rest.

If you were the spouse who kept the peace in the marriage, zip your lips during the haggling. And lose the phone if you're tempted to call your husband and offer: "You can have the house, as long as we can remain friends."

Preserve all evidence, no matter how much you want to pulverize your hard drive. Tammy got into her husband's AOL account and filed away the details of his affair with the mother of their son's classmate. She even discovered websites where they'd posted nudie photos of themselves in search of other couples to swing with.

The judge was not rotfl.[9]

Jackie made copies of the child support checks on which her husband had scrawled **BLOODSUCKER** on the memo line.

Lucy printed out a ream of e-mails between her husband, Barry, and "Candi69@hotmail.com," all about the new Hyundai that Candi wanted Barry to buy for her, and their plans for a rendezvous in "Fuckapulco."

The judge was not lhao.[10]

[9] Rolling on the floor laughing
[10] Laughing his ass off

If *your* husband's Hyundai whore is clamoring to sport a diamond, eventually he'll settle up just to shut her up. So hold out for the antique Aubusson rug. While you're waiting, take Xanax as needed.

Triple the dose if he refuses to leave the house. This is a legal ploy. When Michelle caught her husband canoodling with the Czech nanny, she ordered him out. Instead, he demanded $250,000 from her family's business. Neither is budging. Michelle shipped Zdenka back to Bratislava, while she and her husband remain entrenched in separate bedrooms in the same house. Meanwhile, each posted a "recently divorced" profile on jdate.com.

For court appearances, leave your Chanel suit and Louis Vuitton bag at home, even the knockoffs. And lose a quick ten pounds on a cleansing fast. If your clothing is hanging off you, the judge may want to know where your next meal is coming from. Better yet if you can dig up your old maternity jumper.

Hold out for an eleventh-hour fold. Diane was rummaging through the attic for a moth-eaten outfit when her lawyer called at 10:59 the night before her trial. Her husband agreed to give her half the money he'd invested in state-of-the-art breast implants for Amber, the topless dancer. Plus the house, the Mercedes, the 401(K), and

the bronzed baby shoes.
    Too bad she didn't get his balls.
    Amber kept her cleavage.

LET'S REVIEW:
WHAT YOU NOW KNOW

✓ Enough matrimonial law to pass the bar exam.

✓ About your divorce lawyer: the last person you'd have dinner with may just be your new best friend.

✓ About your husband: the man you shared your life with is your new EX-friend.

✓ In his mind, you and your attorney are responsible for all the world's ills. Including Hurricane Katrina. And his ulcer. You bastards.

✓ So why should he care if you can't pay the electric bill?

✓ How long Con Edison will wait before shutting you off.

✓ Divorce is a grown-up game of "chicken." Don't let him ruffle your feathers.

✓ Where those missing assets went. Amber is wearing them.

- ✓ That ho sent him an e-mail that said, "Make sure your wife is out of the house before I come over."

- ✓ The judge was very annoyed. >: - (

- ✓ An average serving of pad Thai racks up 603 calories, 30 grams of fat, and 2,100 mg of sodium.

- ✓ Your lawyer's fees equal the down payment on a luxury three-bedroom condo.

- ✓ Possibly more if you sleep with him.

- ✓ Unless he's willing to work pro boner.

- ✓ You can't take the brat out of Bratislava.

- ✓ The generic name for Xanax is alprazolam.

PHASE IV:
Ciao, Babe

The divorce is under way, and you're ready to make a fresh start. Begin your new life by performing an exorcism: rid the house of your ex's flotsam, funk, and evaporated sweat.

The New Age way to banish his negative chi[11] is known as smudging. After Meredith's husband moved out, her best friend arrived with a bundle of sage boughs. She lit them and waved the avenging smoke throughout the house. The fumes drove his evil spirit far, far away. It was last seen wreaking havoc in Australia.

Carol gutted her home down to the floorboards. Everything her ex had ever grazed, leaned against, or sneezed on was demolished and turned into landfill. She rebuilt a virgin palace. Then again, she got a kick-ass settlement.

We found that a new Posturepedic and 400-count Egyptian cotton sheets can do the trick more economically. (But

---

[11] Life force. In his case, demons. Think Linda Blair in *The Exorcist*, but with far less projectile vomiting.

don't cheap out and buy a twin—because there's always hope.)

Then there's the matter of his yellowed BVDs. Dump them, and be sure to wear rubber gloves. While you're at it, scrub down the bureau drawers that his clothing once touched, line them with contact paper, and spread out your stuff. Toss the ties festooned with tiny golf clubs and commandeer the closets. Empty his side of the medicine cabinet and replace his Metamucil with a tub of green mud masque.

Febreze the house. He's outta here.

Stick a fork in him: he's done

Much like a kid who has gone off to college, your husband left behind anything he didn't need. His Cosby sweaters and moldering bar mitzvah album do not flow with the pared-down, feng-shui'd lifestyle he now shares with the thirty-year-old tarot card reader. You'll want to purge them, along with his comic books, Herman's Hermits LPs, and Twelve-Step Guide. Shred his baseball card collection in the Cuisinart. Torch his old love letters, and immediately trash that Hawaiian honeymoon photo of him posing next to the luau pig.

On second thought, sell the LPs on eBay.

Give him a deadline for removing his crud. In the meantime, hurl it into Hefty bags. After the deadline comes and goes, have Goodwill pick up his residue. Keep the receipt for a tax deduction.

Your home is still tainted by smut and toxic waste, everywhere you look. Rent a hazmat suit, gas mask, and Dumpster. Let the decontamination begin.

1. Oust the pictures of your ex that continue to pollute the living room. Later on, when you're dating, potential boyfriends will not be charmed by that adorable shot of the pudgy Little Leaguer minus his two front teeth—unless you're prepared to lie and say it's your son. Here are a few creative solutions that even involve recycling:

A) Carefully cut him out of each photo and mail him twenty-one tiny versions of his decapitated head. Slightly disturbed, totally satisfying.
B) Give his pictures to the NRA to distribute to rednecks for target practice.
C) Send his latest girlfriend all the photos that show off either his gut or his bald spot, or if you're really lucky, both in one shot.
D) Always keep the frames.

2. Your husband's bacteria and fungi are clinging to the master bedroom. *Pee-ew!* They lurk in the lamp shades, Levolors, and air-conditioning ducts. The room cries out for fumigation and renovation. Try these helpful household hints:

A) Hire a cleaning service—or the EPA—to expunge all forensic evidence of his twenty-five-year presence. This includes bellybutton lint, chest hairs, toe jam, and dandruff flakes.

B) Have the crew Lysol the bathroom for earwax, petrified tooth tartar, and those sticky yellow stains from all the times he missed the toilet bowl.

C) Sanitize the bedroom with a fresh coat of paint. Wild Orchid.

D) If he took his dresser and nightstand, fill the empty space with a treadmill. Use it every night. *It* doesn't need Viagra.

E) Your bedroom still seems vacant without him? Buy a giant fern.

F) The best way to reclaim your bed: have sex with another man in it. Arrange to do this on your ex's fiftieth. As you finish, think: *Happy Birthday, Fred. Yessssss!*

3. Your daughter has made it clear that she doesn't want the doomed karma oozing from your wedding dress and engagement ring. You are free to dispose of these relics and raise a little extra cash— or at least take them as a write-off. The following strategies would make your accountant proud:

A) Remove the diamond from its band and replace it with polished glass ($1.99). Then mail the ring to your ex with an Emily Post etiquette note offering it for his next wife. Sell the real stone for whatever it's worth.

B) Hawk your wedding rings on eBay. You'll rake in enough to splurge on the works: highlights, facial, massage, mani-pedi, body scrub, seaweed wrap. Throw in the gown and tiara, and treat yourself to eyelash extensions.

C) If spite is your cup of tea, take a stroll in a nearby park and choose a nice-looking home-less couple. Give them his grandmother's heir-loom ring. You'll find this charitable gesture deeply rewarding.

D) Be a philanthropist. Donate your diamond ring to the rummage sale for your niece's cheerlead-ing squad. They could *totally* use it to buy, like, ALL their airfares to the finals!

4. You were never crazy about that wedding picture in which your ex and his best man staggered onto the stage and did their boozy, frat-house rendition of "Wild Thing." Don't miss this opportunity to hack it up and, while you're at it, the whole album. Here are a few rainy day arts-and-crafts activities:

A) Invite your best friend over with her sharpest pair of scissors. You provide the wine. Take turns cutting up everyone you hate in the album, page by page.

B) Ditch the scissors and verbally cut up all of his relatives. Then draw facial hair and eye patches on everyone with a Sharpie marker.

C) Rip the album apart with your bare hands. Afterwards, make sure to schedule a manicure appointment.

D) Leave it in the attic in case your children ever want to see evidence that their father once had hair. And a waistline.

Damn that feels good. You want more, don't you? Yeah, you do.

Shopping for justice

Yes, you'd feel a lot better if your ex fell head first down a flight of stairs and wound up in a full body cast, in traction, only to be devoured by a raging colony of pubic lice under the plaster. Or maybe his girlfriend's liposuction could backfire, so all the fat in her entire body is now dimpling her thighs and her breasts have shrunk from a DD to an AA. Sweet. If fate does not comply, you can take these therapeutic steps:

Invite your most fashion-forward friend to go through your closet and help you part with your Laura Ashley dresses, fuzzy mop slippers, and reindeer sweaters. Move those Easy Spirit clodhoppers to a high shelf, way in the back. Better yet, burn them—before someone nominates you for *What Not to Wear.*

If you have a daughter age seventeen or older, take her shopping for new threads. For *you.* (If you don't possess this valuable resource, borrow a friend's daughter.) She'll teach you the difference between soccer-mom stodgy and single-mom sexy, guiding you in your image transition from:

Talbots to Banana Republic

L.L.Bean to J.Crew

Eileen Fisher to Marc Jacobs

HRC[12] to SJP[13]

Give her carte blanche to replace your potato-sack *shmatas* with lace-trimmed tanks and form-fitted skirts. And don't balk when she substitutes fuck-me boots for your clogs.

As your personal shopper, she'll insist that you trade in your stretched-out Playtex Living Bras for lacy black pushups. Make sure to stuff a pair of silicone "chicken cutlets" inside.

The Shalimar your ex bought you for every birthday will now make you gag. Toss it, and invite all the women in your office to accompany you to the fragrance counter at lunchtime to choose a new scent that says, "Sniff me. You know you want to."

Get a free makeover at a department store. Arrange to meet a friend afterwards for martinis at the see-and-be-seen bar in town. Don't waste a gorgeous moment.

Say *sayonara* to your ruffled flannel nightgowns with the little hearts and flowers—the ones you wore every night for the past twenty-five years—and replace them with *anything*. Or nothing. Promise that even on the coldest night, in the deepest throes of the flu, you will never don such garments again.

Throw yourself a birthday bash, and make sure there's only one candle on the cake. In lieu of gifts, ask

[12] Hillary Rodham Clinton
[13] Sarah Jessica Parker

each of your girlfriends to bring you a single, straight male who didn't just escape from an asylum for the criminally insane or a fat farm.

Look at the bright side of being single on Valentine's Day. Instead of scarfing down the truffles in that Russell Stover Deluxe your ex always gave you, now you can imagine them puckering his girlfriend with cellulite and peppering her with zits.

Don't be a wallflower on dreaded V-Day. Until your heartthrob comes along, make a pact with a single girlfriend to exchange lingerie, especially a satin thong that says **Tease Me** or **Please Me.** Boyfriend or no, wear it. In case you get hit by a bus.

Announce to your ex that he has won full custody of the dog. Practice sounding wistful, yet generous. (You'll even throw in the leash.) When you look outside at 6:30 a.m. and it's raining, think of him, smile, roll over, and go back to sleep.

Treat yourself to a flat-screen TV, and to help pay for it, cut your cable bill in half by getting rid of all those sports and skin channels. On second thought, keep the porn.

Rent *The First Wives Club* and roar. Repeat as necessary.

Lucky you: he left behind his priceless collection of Flesh-Eating Zombie DVDs. Toss 'em, and buy yourself all six seasons of *Sex and the City*.

Rejoice and redecorate. Now's your chance to get rid of his grandmother's clunky Victorian claw-footed table, and the bedspread his aunt Selma created in Beginner Crochet at the condo rec center. Hallelujah!

Sell them on craigslist, along with his leatherette BarcaLounger. Give your ad a catchy title to attract buyers, something like, "My ex is pond scum. Buy his shit."

Go blonde.

Solo on Saturday night

You call your single girlfriends, each and every one of them, but they've all lined up dates through match.com. You ring up your best married friend and whine. She says, "You think you have it bad? I'm having dinner with my aunt in the Alzheimer's unit tonight." You beg to tag along, but she thinks you're joking.

You buzz your daughter's cell for the fourth time that day. After all, weekend minutes are free. She sees your caller ID and grumbles, "What now?" You improvise a quick excuse, advising her to drive carefully because it's raining. Well, it *is*.

When your computer is your only reliable companion, consider a few of our favorite dates:

- Log onto awfulplasticsurgery.com and check out the bad, the worse, and the ugly of celebrity make-overs. Learn all about Melanie Griffith's lip collagen disaster and why Courtney Love looks like she's hoarding chestnuts in her cheeks. We like to begin our search with the Bad Boob Job Hall of Fame.
- Then join the fans who post notes to the webmaster, like: "Good job spotting Natalie Portman's stream-lined nose!" Once you've exhausted the archives, more entertainment awaits at goodplasticsurgery.com. (Warning: these sites are addictive.)

- When you're feeling more cerebral, click on www.isc.ro for a rousing match of Internet Scrabble. Don't spend too much time wondering who the other players are, and why this is their choice of activity on a Saturday night. Judge not, ladies.

- There's nothing like a little retail therapy to help you forget your woes. Indulge in an online shopping spree for jeans, shoes, handbags—you name it—at bluefly, eluxury, yoox, overstock, and zappos. Our favorite is pamperedpassions.com for va-va-va-voom Italian lingerie. You'll feel like Sophia Loren back in the day.

- Once you've hit your credit limit, opt for celebrity bashing—it's free. Gofugyourself.com features wardrobe malfunctions of the rich and famous. Even Scarlett Johansson's celebrated rack, encased in couture, gets dished. Nothing like mocking the impossibly beautiful to make you feel better about your A-cup Wonderbra.

- There's something awfully depressing about settling in with a 1,000-piece puzzle on a Saturday night. Luckily, you can spare a little dignity and do it online at jigzone.com. With hundreds of jigsaws in every difficulty and shape, you'll fill your weekends indefinitely. And just in case you ever have a date, he won't see the evidence of your lonely existence strewn all over the coffee table.

- Check out your teenage son's myspace page. Read all about the rager[14] he threw last weekend, and how the cops broke it up because everybody got crunked.[15] While you were at a serenity retreat with your divorce support group.

IT'S 5 O'CLOCK SOMEWHERE

We discovered that a tumbler of single-malt scotch can be a pleasant antidote to those lonely evenings spent with Jerry, Kramer, George, et al. Especially when you're clean out of NyQuil. Watch out, however, if you find yourself waiting for the minute hand to hit 4:59 so you can pour your second drink. More than one a night, we learned, does nothing but tighten the waistband on your sexy new True Religion jeans. Before you know it, your stomach is bulging over the belt like a muffin top. And you don't like that. So fill a generous Thermos, and eighty-six the bottle.

---

[14] Wild inebriated party that turns your house into a parking lot
[15] Crazy + drunk

The rabbit habit

What would it take to get you purring again? Most self-help books prescribe bubble baths. But is squeaky-clean really what you long for? We recommend a guy who whispers in your ear, "I'll do whatever you want for as long as you want."

Meet BOB.[16]

Everybody has dated him. The best thing about BOB: he's always up for you. He comes in infinite shapes, sizes, and speeds, AC/DC or AA. When you're with him, you can skip the mascara and let your armpits sprout. Come as you are.

All you need is a tube of Astroglide and an Energizer twelve-pack by your bedside. Unless you prefer high-voltage orgasms, in which case you'll want an electrical outlet.

Maureen spends fifteen minutes of quality time with BOB before a date. "It takes the edge off," she explains. "I can think before I jump into bed with someone. If you have half a sandwich before a party, you'll resist dessert. Sex is just like food."

Suzie likes the convenience. "I don't have to cook for him or talk to him, and it's over when I want it to be." On the other hand, the buzzing causes her Akita to bark relentlessly.

The two best sellers at babeland.com are made in Japan. The Hitachi Magic Wand is a plug-in massager

[16] Battery Operated Boyfriend

that has "the best word of mouth of any vibrator," according to Babeland co-founder Claire Cavanah. The cordless Rabbit Habit has three functions:

1) a twirling dildo
2) a band of pearly balls that tumble and roll
3) a special bunny attachment with pulsing ears that will drive you wild.

When was the last time your ex did all that for you?

The iBuzz is the newest and sexiest accessory for your iPod. It connects to any mp3 player and vibrates in time to your favorite tunes. Like "Satisfaction."

For portability, Cavanah recommends the Pocket Rocket, which you can carry in your purse for roadside emergencies. It's no bigger than a lipstick, but loads more fun.

Everybody has her preference. Danielle is fond of a G-string with a leather pouch containing a small, vibrating egg. Kate swore by the Tongue until it shorted out during a blizzard, leaving her marooned for three days with nothing but porn-on-demand.

She also appreciates the packaging at mypleasure.com. A discreet, unmarked carton arrives. Inside, her new playmate is wrapped in pink cellophane with a matching bow. It's the gift that keeps on giving.

Judy favors the Water Dancer, a small massager that takes one tiny AAA battery. She doesn't just use it in the tub. "I throw it in my bag and take it everywhere," she says. "If I accidentally leave it on my nightstand and the kids see it, I say, 'That's for when Mommy's neck hurts.'"

Sex toys are the new Tupperware. Host a party for your friends, then pick out a slew of freebies for yourself. At a recent soiree, Judy noticed that everyone was grabbing up the Dolphin—a waterproof cousin of the Rabbit. "I wanted to try all kinds of new things that I'd never thought about before," she says. "Getting divorced is the best thing that ever happened to my sex life."

Yippee! The holidays are here again

You're done with your wasband,[17] but you still receive his dental reminders and Hazelden alumni updates. And even though you mark his mail "Deceased—Return to Sender," he continues to slither back into your life, especially when he's feeling nostalgic. These occasions may include, but are not limited to: Thanksgiving, Christmas, Martin Luther King Day, April Fools', Election Day, Purim. Also, dinnertime.

What should you do when he sticks his foot in the door? Any of the following responses are effective.

1. You return from work to find that the babysitter has been sent home and your ex is ensconced on your couch with a bag of Cheetos, watching *SpongeBob SquarePants* with the kids. He casually greets you, belches, and asks what's for supper.

    A) Tell him you're going out for mojitos with Julio, your tango instructor. No need to mention that Julio is on Medicare. And gay.
    B) Remark that the Cheetos have nestled in nicely around his waistline.
    C) Change the locks.
    D) Vacuum the sofa.

[17] Was husband

2. Six months after he moves out, he sends an e-mail suggesting that it would be "warm and cozy" for the family to be together for Christmas at your place.

    A) Forward him the children's Dear Santa wish lists and thank him in advance for his generous offer.

    B) Assign him the job of cooking the turkey, ham, mashed potatoes, Brussels sprouts, creamed onions, and pecan pie. Graciously volunteer to warm everything up.

    C) Instruct him to buy the tree, haul it into the living room, put up the ladder, string the lights, fill the stockings, hang the wreaths, and return when it's time to take everything down.

    D) Convert to Judaism.

LET'S REVIEW:
WHAT YOU NOW KNOW

✓ Your husband will treat you like a rental storage bin.

✓ How to smudge him out.

✓ And for $5.95 you can pick up a smudge stick at your local health food store.

✓ A bleach and water solution works wonders on old pee stains.

✓ How to remove a diamond from a prong setting.

✓ A belted trench looks better than a puffy ski parka.

✓ There are many ways to stuff chicken cutlets.

✓ Even Grandma Pearl doesn't want your old Lanz nighties.

✓ A Saturday night spent online is a lot less fattening than a pint of Double Fudge Brownie.

- ✓ Besides, how else would you learn that in her lacy blue gown, Beyoncé's breasts were pushed high enough to rest a drink on?

- ✓ The beeper number of a wine merchant who delivers. Even on Sundays.

- ✓ Your ex will repeat on you like a greasy chili dog with jalapeños and onions.

- ✓ A Christmas tree is a bitch to carry in by yourself.

- ✓ Your iPod is way cooler than you thought.

- ✓ Never use an electrical appliance in the bathtub.

PHASE V:
Manhunt

*Y*ou're feeling sexy again. But you'd feel even better if somebody, i.e. a man, would just confirm that. Welcome to the brave new world of Dating, Act II.

Be forewarned: dating at midlife is nothing like when you were in your twenties. The first time around, you frolicked in an infinity pool full of cute young guys with high hopes, clean slates, and more importantly, hair. Now the guys are weary, leery, war-torn, and resemble the Pillsbury Doughboy. Plus there is no pool. Just a small puddle. Sometimes it seems more like a swamp.

Caution. You are now a goddess to every man twenty years older than you. Retirees who wear their pants hiked up to their armpits will hit on you. This may seem flattering at first, but trust us: it wears thin fast. Now that your husband is doing the samba with a Paris-Lindsay-Britney look-alike, or the lap dancer he met in Atlantic City, or the marriage counselor the two of you were seeing, what you need more than anything else is a man who will make you feel gorgeous and desirable again. He's out there, and willing to oblige.

How do you go about finding him? Grab your tranquilizer darts and let the safari begin.

The fix-up date: don't hold your breath

The bad news is, it's hard to get one. The instant someone's husband so much as packs a suitcase, he is deluged by an eager phalanx of sisters and aunts, the church choir and the PTA, not to mention the dental hygienist, all vying to set him up with "wonderful women." For some reason, your name is never on their matchmaking lists.

You, on the other hand, will badger everyone you know to dredge up even one heterosexual male who is younger than your grandfather, resides in the Western hemisphere, and hasn't done time (for anything worse than insider trading). Your friends, desperate to help, will come up with inspired suggestions like these:

"My husband's podiatrist is available, but if you only knew what he did to his ex-wife. . . ."

You picture dismembered feet in his basement, and move on.

"I have a guy you could date for practice, but he's very messed up. Promise that you won't get involved with him."

You may be rusty, but your time is still of some value.

"I know a really fit, trim guy in his mid-fifties. He looks forty. And the best thing is, he comes with no baggage. He's never been married."

Keep in mind, there's a reason for everything.

"How about my brother? Okay, he has his issues, but everyone has issues."

Yeah, so what if he's a methadone addict?

"I want you to be the next person I fix my friend Brad up with. He adores football, loves a good cigar, and vacations in Vegas twice a year."

You are allergic to smoke, attend the opera religiously, and are saving up for a garden tour of Europe. The fact that you and Brad are both divorced, and both know her, does not a relationship make.

The widower: America's most wanted

Somewhere in your suspicious psyche, you're convinced that every divorced man committed a dastardly deed to end his marriage. Not so for the saintly widower. He's out there through no fault of his own. This guy is the Hope Diamond in a world full of cubic zirconium.

Unfortunately, gazillions of other divorced women think the same way. Watch that you don't get trampled by the casserole brigade. The freshly minted widower gets snatched up before his wife's body turns cold. We've seen it happen at funeral parlors and *shivah* calls. Some women routinely check the obits and show up at the cemetery, all dolled up.

As a friend in Florida observed, "Every time a wife dies, a star is born."

If you do have the rare good luck to nab a widower, be prepared to mop up his tears on the first date, and beware the ghost of the deceased. Remember the movie *Rebecca*? Don't be surprised if there's a life-sized portrait of Saint Cookie, sizing you up from her perch above the mantle. It will stay there forever if his children have anything to say about it, and they will.

The Internet: cracking the code

So what's a girl to do? That ad you answered in the newspaper personals produced Bruce, a lifelong bachelor who rhapsodized about his cat, Misty, his harp, and his love of eighteenth-century French ball gowns. Speed dating was like musical chairs from hell, and you lost. You *thought* you accepted a dinner invitation from Sven, the Scandinavian tennis pro. Instead you got stuck with Seymour, the gastric-bypass candidate who had fish breath.

Unless you work in a urologist's office or some other male milieu, your quest will inevitably take you into cyberspace. Six months after Lisa's husband moved out, she posted a profile and presto: her face popped up on the screens of hundreds of male subscribers. The next day she opened e-mails from all over the eastern seaboard. Within a week she was in wrist splints, nursing a vicious case of carpal tunnel syndrome.

Yes, they're out there, plenty of them. But their profiles are a crock of cow dung. Here's a guide to what guys write, and what they *really* mean.

The horny

"The instant we look into each other's eyes, we will know if that special chemistry is there."

Translation: He has zero interest in getting to know you.

"I know my way around a wine list and the nape of a beautiful neck."

He hasn't been laid in years.

"Can you be intimate and passionate for hours and hours?"

Can you handle a one-night stand? Do you mind if it lasts ten minutes?

"My date should enjoy soft, wet, delicious kisses."

He thinks you'd be excited by the image of a total stranger slobbering all over your face. Yum.

"31-year-old man, looking for women 45 to 60."

Don't be flattered. He assumes older women are sex-starved and grateful.

"I don't believe in long-distance relationships."

He's all about the booty call.

Commitment-phobes

"I'm searching for my soul mate."

He's been out there for a long time, and will remain there.

"Would like to meet a woman who is non-demanding."

He has intimacy issues. And wants to sleep around.

"I'm looking for a woman who likes her own space."

And will stay out of his.

"Seeking a woman who does not NEED a man in her life, but who WANTS a man in her life."

He won't be there for you. But you can be there for him, if you'd like.

"I possess the ability to listen."

Note: He does not say he avails himself of this ability.

The underemployed

"I quit the rat race."

He spends his days in an overstuffed armchair at Barnes & Noble, reading Hustler *for free.*

"I'm semi-retired, doing consulting work."

He occasionally gets up from the chair to flip through the Start Your Own Business shelf.

"I am Executive Vice-President of Strategic Planning for a major corporation."

He's self-employed in some cockamamie business, headquartered in his basement.

He lists a career in "financial services."

He drives a limo for CEOs.

"Please don't respond if you're just looking for a free meal."

Prepare for a beverage date at 7-Eleven.

Geeks, neurotics, and big fat liars

"I'd like to meet a woman who is nonjudgmental."

He bailed on his wife, three kids and basset hound—for the Swedish au pair.

He describes his body type as "about average."

He only looks in the mirror on the medicine cabinet.

"I've been told I'm very handsome."

By his mother.

He's pictured in front of a Maserati, or wearing a skipper's cap.

His midlife crisis is still ongoing.

"My hobbies are skydiving, bungee jumping, and alligator wrestling."

Erectile dysfunction.

"R U Here to Meet UR Best Friend, 2 LUV U 4Ever?"

He has the mentality of a thirteen-year-old girl.

"56-year-old man, looking for women 30 to 55."

He's willing to date a woman of any age—except his own. His vanity knows no bounds, but his maturity clearly does.

You now understand the twisted language of Profilese. But there's more hogwash to decode: his "personal stats" section. This one's easy—just do the math:

Subtract three inches from his height.

Double his weight.

Halve his income.

Add a decade to his age.

Off the beaten path

While everybody else is clicking away on match.com, why not think outside the box and come up with your own creative ways of meeting men? Try these detours if the information highway is backed up:

- Before you pay your final legal bill, needle your divorce lawyer to introduce you to a male client. If he chooses not to see this as part of his job, pay up anyway. But reappear frequently in his reception area, looking hot. After all, you have loose ends to tie up.
- Be the only single woman who boldly ventures from her home on Valentine's Day. Wiggle your way into a high-end restaurant, where you'll find a line-up of guys dining at the bar. You can be sure that no attached man is among them. Pull up a stool and say hello to Mr. Lonelyheart.
- Sign up for a "no girls allowed" adult ed class. You can bet you'll be the only female student in Cooking for Morons or Advanced Auto Repair. Note: must actually be prepared to learn something about auto repair and maybe even touch grease.
- Stand around The Home Depot admiring the screwdrivers. Just be careful not to get trapped in a

conversation *about* screwdrivers.

• Look intensely absorbed (but stunning) as you browse the Military History section at Borders.

• Get a job in a pool hall.

• Stroll into any steak house at feeding time.

LET'S REVIEW:
WHAT YOU NOW KNOW

✓ Your friends don't know any single men.
   Except losers.

✓ Speaking of which, the podiatrist[18] has
   dates lined up through Labor Day.

✓ Never attend a funeral without makeup.

✓ And black is flattering to every woman.

✓ Anyone named Bruce is probably gay.

✓ It's always Seymour who calls, never Sven.

✓ Internet dating will leave you wondering
   if the men are recruited straight out of
   mental institutions.

✓ Re: those profiles. Read between the lines.
   BTW, you won't believe the lines you'll
   read.

✓ Keep a calculator handy.

✓ Men don't know from full-length mirrors.

---

[18] {:- wears a toupee

✓ Your divorce lawyer has single guys' phone numbers in his PDA, lots of them.

✓ Any male seated next to an empty barstool is up for grabs on Valentine's Day.

✓ You need a lug wrench, a c-clamp, and a small bungee cord to replace your brake pads.

✓ Men can be found near books about war.

✓ And platters of aged porterhouse.

PHASE VI:

Dating in the New Millennium

*Y*ou spent most of your adult life married to your ex. The end result: you know nothing about men, and even less about dating them. Remember the last time you went out on a date? It was a different century!

A year ago, your night table was crammed with self-help books that promised to save your marriage. And where did that get you? Here, today, memorizing *The Rules* and *Dating for Dummies*, and studiously marking passages with your yellow highlighter. Someday you'll get back to Oprah's Book Club List, but for now these are required reading.

You grill your daughter about when to return a guy's call, what to wear, how to open a text message. You forward his Internet profile for her approval. She points out that he's a dead ringer for the Unabomber and asks if you arrived on the planet yesterday. With great condescension, she pronounces you "dating-autistic" and delivers a painfully elementary lecture on the how-to's of handling men. Take notes.

Imagine that you were cryogenically frozen twenty-five years ago and just thawed out. That's how you seem to her. But you'll catch up. Just take our crash course on dating etiquette, AD 2008.

Welcome back.

Intro to chemistry

Now that your marriage has fizzled, you can't wait to pop a few Roman candles and bottle rockets. Caution: fireworks on a first date can be harmful to your health. Your mother was dead-on when she warned that they could blind you. (See Phase VII, Mr. Wrong.)

On the other hand, it's reasonable to expect a modest spark—or at least not to spend the entire evening planning your escape, only to go home nauseous. Cut it short if you encounter any of these scenarios:

Over dirty martinis, you learn way more than you'd ever want to know about his postnasal drip, including all

the details of his visit to the ear-nose-and-throat special-
ist, who only hours earlier vacuumed the mucus out of
his nostrils.

You meet on a blustery day, and his full head of
rather attractive, snowy white hair unravels in the wind
like cotton candy, revealing a twelve-inch comb-over.

You've arranged to meet your blind date at a restaurant
at 8 p.m. You arrive at 7:55 to find him already seated at
the table. He doesn't stand up when you approach, not
even to shake your hand. You are correct in assuming any
or all of the following:

    A) At 5'3" in heels, you will tower over him.

    B) His belly, wedged under the table, is shockingly
       large.

    C) He has no manners.

    D) He's wearing socks with sandals.

    E) He's hiding a whopper hard-on.

He offers you the banquette seat against the mirrored
wall, and you're thrilled that he's such a gentleman. For
the remainder of the evening, you're unable to make
eye contact as he gazes adoringly at his own reflection.

He sports an ascot and spends the entire date enlight-
ening you about his favorite topic: the history of the
croissant. *Mon dieu*.

He eats his entire meal, and some of yours, with his

hands—including the tuna salad.

During dinner, he diagrams the path of his kidney stone, which has ping-ponged out of his urethra and into his bladder. He tops this with the news that he's wearing a testosterone patch. On his tush.

Willing to give him another chance, you agree to a second date, on which he hocks a loogy into his napkin and inspects his phlegm.

Bad news. It's yellow.

Big man on campus

Remember those pizza-faced rejects—you know, with the acne that's both red and white—who couldn't get to first base in high school? Now they're the middle-aged make-out kings. Including the ones who grew up to be trolls.

This annoying development stems from two deplorable social trends:

1. These men are cocky due to the favorable supply-and-demand ratio. In the words of one divorced BMOC: "Women are like buses. Another one comes along every fifteen minutes."

2. They're lusty because they're incapable of sustaining a relationship long enough to make it into the bedroom.

FIRST DATE DON'TS

Memorize these taboos if you don't want to blow it. On the other hand, if you instantly loathe him and are looking for an exit route, most of the following tactics will work quite nicely indeed.

DON'T boast about your legal strategy to snag 80 percent of the marital assets.

DON'T badger him with questions like, "So why *did* your marriage end? You were shtupping the babysitter, right? Right?"

DON'T warn him that if you start weeping over the guacamole, it's only because you forgot to refill your Zoloft prescription.

DON'T mention that you're looking for a long-term, committed, monogamous relationship. Or for a friend.

DON'T complain about how your ex used to stink up the bathroom.

DON'T tell amusing tales about all the other cretins you've dated.

DON'T ask him if he's *really* fifty-nine, or demand to see his driver's license. Just Google him later.

DON'T get totally bombed. Or barf on his shoe.

DON'T spend the evening discussing your hysterectomy, or for that matter, vaginal dryness.

DON'T expound on your theory that all men are actually scientifically less evolved than women.

DON'T describe the panties you're wearing, unless you plan to show, tell, and more.

So be prepared for the occasional lech. For instance, after you meet for the first time at a restaurant for lunch, he leans down to say good-bye, and you offer your cheek. Undeterred, he twists your head around and sucks half your face with his gaping mouth. You're not sure if he's yawning, kissing you, or practicing CPR. Then he insists on seeing you home "safely" in a taxi, where he attempts to unbutton your shirt.

How much touchy-feely stuff is okay on a first date? None, if it involves being mauled at 40 mph in a back seat full of piney freshness. And enough is enough if you wake up the next morning with a hangover and a neck full of hickeys. That wasn't even cool when you were twenty-five.

Dishonesty is the best policy

You've dated him a couple of times, and it's just not happening. But he's so besotted that he invites you to a Neil Diamond concert—front row! You lucky girl. You'd rather stay home and watch South Park *with your kids. How do you bow out? It could be harder than you think.*

Whatever you do, never bring up his age as an objection. His seventy-five to your fifty-three is not something you should mention. And it won't soften the blow to ask how he'd like to date a ninety-seven-year-old woman, which would be the equivalent age gap.

The truth will *not* set you free. Abby and Bill clicked online, but in the flesh, she was repelled by his bulging gut and brown fangs,[19] which he'd Photoshopped out of his Internet pics. The next day she IM'd him: *"You're a great guy, but I think we just want different things."* Within hours he flooded her e-mail box with lesbian pornography.

"Platonic" is Greek to him. Patty went out with a man who fatally resembled her friend Kristen's ex-husband. When he called for a second date, Patty explained that she just wanted to be friends. "Sure," he agreed. "But

[19] **:-E** bucktoothed vampire

could there be a sexual component to the friendship?"
Apparently there *is* such a thing as a stupid question.

Bottom line: stop with the tactful explanations that piss everybody off. Just say you're busy. This will allow him to dismiss you as a jerk and move on. Besides, if you don't know how to lie, you have no business dating.

E I E I Owe?

This is a reading comprehension test. Study the passage below and answer to the best of your ability.

Audrey met Howard through match.com. On their first date, breakfast at a diner, he packed away a cheese omelet with ham, sausage, bacon, and hash browns. Plus a side of silver-dollar pancakes. She had a muffin and coffee. Howard split the tab, announcing that each owed $17.01.

Howard next invited Audrey out for a day on his boat, instructing her to bring the sandwiches because he was "springing for the gas." The pattern continued, with Howard expecting Audrey to go halvsies at museums, movies, and every time he parked his car in a lot.

Audrey continued to see Howard, but only as friends. One evening at Denny's, he grabbed the check with a flourish. Later, while watching TV at her place, he suddenly flipped up her skirt and became a cunning linguist.

Mark each of the following statements true or false.

___ Howard was an Atkins flunkout.

___ This relationship should have ended after breakfast.

___ Howard could have found a free parking space on the street.

___ Audrey should have made him a knuckle sandwich and charged him double.

___ Still, she didn't mind being dessert.

Correct answers: all are true. But more important, Audrey needs to get off match.com. Today.

Losing your second virginity

ASAP

After fifteen years of married life, you're in a hurry to break the sex barrier and prove that you still have your mojo.

You're itching to make your ex's thirty-year-old slore[20] look like a nun in comparison.

You're dying to go a little wild—with someone other than a plastic motorized rabbit.

The first question every newly sprung woman asks is, "How long do I have to wait before I can sleep with him?" The answer depends on what you're looking for.

- A roll in the hay: as soon as you get your Brazilian bikini wax.
- A little romance: three weeks, so you can savor the foreplay. When was the last time you French-kissed in the rain, in the middle of the sidewalk?
- A long-term relationship: until you really know him, because once you have sex with him—if it's good—your perspective will fly out the window. He could be Hannibal Lecter, and you'd dreamily tell your friends, "He's a keeper."

(Note: regardless of whether it's love or lust, do not try to "entice" him to stay overnight by dangling the possibil-

[20] Slut/whore hybrid

ity of frozen, whole-wheat, low-cal, fiber-filled waffles in the morning. With sugar-free syrup. Take our word for it.)

Twenty-first century male primate behavior

Thanks to a gender ratio that's dangerously out of whack, many midlife BMOCs behave like kids in a candy store. They'll sleep with you on Friday night and with Jennifer or Jessica on Saturday. This privileged status applies to all men. They don't even have to be employed, straight, mentally competent, use deodorant, or weigh less than 400 pounds.

Here's what you want to know:

Q: *Can I insist on a sexually exclusive relationship?*

A: Absolutely.

Q: *When do I bring it up?*

A: Just before he's ready to come.

Remedial Sex Ed

The next big question on women's minds goes something like this: "But I haven't had great sex in years! Besides, he says I'm the only one. Do we *really* have to use a condom?"

The answer is always YES. And if he doesn't have one handy, do not suggest tin foil as a homespun alternative.

The same goes for Ziploc sandwich bags. And don't waste your time trying to Purell his penis.

At this point, most sixteen-year-old girls know more about protection than you do. Tina was separated for less than a year when she dove into a torrid love affair. She and her boyfriend got tested for AIDS and other STDs, which happily resulted in unlimited, unprotected sex.

One night Tina rolled over in his bed and felt something tangled up in her toes. She reached between the sheets and pulled up a lavender thong that she'd never seen before. Blood tests are great, but condoms provide the only real protection against liars. And lavender thongs.

Surprise: Mommy is a woman

Your kids are okay with their fifty-three-year-old father living with the twenty-nine-year-old personal trainer he got personal with at the gym. But you must be saintly and virginal. To your children, you're Mother Teresa—married only to God or their father.

After twenty years of wearing your husband's old Zeta Psi T-shirts, size XXL, you're newly sporting a young, trendy look. Don't get too extreme with the Abercrombie minis, footless tights, and platform flip-flops. When Holly got decked out one evening, her teenage son frowned at her getup and asked, "Is there a dance at the middle school tonight?"

You've gone waaaay far if your eighteen-year-old daughter yanks on the belly chain you bought at Claire's, and says you look like a skank.[21]

Don't forget that your college freshman still thinks you live to roast chicken. Wendy's son popped home unexpectedly, laundry bags and roommates in tow, only to find his mom straddling her boyfriend's lap in the kitchen. That's why divorced women move into buildings with doormen and avoid the ground floor.

---

[21] "A slutty, dirty girl who dresses so nasty and has roots and acne and looks like she has a venereal disease."

Your fifteen-year-old daughter used to spend every Saturday night at her best friend's house. Now that you're dating steadily, she's suddenly declared it "homework night" and needs your help with algebra, even though you both know that the last time you solved an equation was in 1979.

Your teenagers may start to act like parents. When Julie stayed out late one night, her kids sat home, worrying. "The nerve of her, keeping us up like this," they fumed. At 1:30 a.m. her son called her cell and offered: "If you've been drinking, I'll pick you up wherever you are—no questions asked."

Don't give your twenty-two-year-old daughter updates about whether you've slept with Ronald yet. Like, too much information. Gross. "Boundaries, Mom, boundaries," we were warned. "It's always good to have one or two."

Don't expect your kids to like any man you date within the first year of your separation. Even if he has his own show on Comedy Central, he's still just a tool[22] to them.

It works both ways. Don't be your boyfriend's first or second post-marriage relationship. You'd cringe if you heard the biting remarks his daughters make when you bend over in your low-rise jeans:

Caitlin: Ew, elderly Britney butt.

[22] A huge teenage insult

Hailey: Nasty. There should be an age limit for those jeans. Diesel should, like, card people when they walk in.

Caitlin: Totally. No one over, like, thirty allowed in unless accompanied by someone with a clue.

Hailey: Oh gross, ew ew, shield your eyes! She's wearing a thong. Like, who does she think she is?

Caitlin: Like, young? Or, like, thin?

Hailey: Totally. Ew. Ew, those pants do not belong on that booty.

Caitlin: Clearly. I think I see the seam splitting. Fat ass.

Hailey: Fat ass.

LET'S REVIEW:
WHAT YOU NOW KNOW

✓ Abort after the shrimp cocktail if your date discusses his acid reflux. Unless you're a gastroenterologist.

✓ Never mention your yeast infection. Even if he's a gynecologist.

✓ DON'T call your therapist from the table.

✓ The croissant was created in 1686 by a Hungarian baker to commemorate a battle with the Turks.

✓ Foundation doesn't cover hickeys. And good luck trying to hide them under a muffler in July.

✓ Men are willing to be just friends, as long as you're willing to have sex with them. Makes sense.

✓ Never, ever go out with cheapskate Howard.

✓ Nothing beats making out on a park bench after fifteen years of wham-bam-thank-you-ma'am.

✓ Always take two Advil before a Brazilian wax.

✓ Blood tests don't lie. But men do.

✓ As does Photoshop.

✓ In the equation $x + 9 = 18 - 2x$, the value of x is 3.

✓ Your boyfriend is SUCH a freaking tool.

✓ Hailey and Caitlin don't like you.

✓ Dressing like a skank only makes it worse.

PHASE VII:
Mr. Wrong

*Y*ou're used to being one-half of a couple, and you liked it that way. Now you're so eager to be with a man—any man—that you're likely to wind up with the wrong man. And believe us, there are plenty of bad bets out there.

Game rules:

1) Beware of men who by age fifty have never married. They'll still be searching at sixty. And seventy. By eighty, they'll find an ex-porn star named Muffy Cumsalot to marry them for their money.

2) Ditto for the career daters who've been divorced or widowed for ten years. They'll hold out until they need someone to change their Depends.

3) Steer clear of the serial polygamists who've tied and untied the knot so many times they could win a Boy Scout medal.

4) Don't get involved if he's only been separated for six months, unless you're willing to be one of his

wild oats. Plus he'll return to his wife's house for Chanukah. All eight days.

5) Never assume a man isn't juggling three other women just because he's 5'2" and hideous. In this market, even Quasimodo could score.

You'll remain fresh prey in the dating world until you learn to recognize the following types:
- *players*
- *married men*
- *guys who aren't emotionally available*
- *men who've been dating for years because nobody else wants them*

Rogues' gallery

Meet the FBI's Most Wanted. On second thought, don't. These bad boys will stir up your deepest fantasies and charm the pants off you, literally. Under no circumstances sleep with one of them—unless all you want is a fling. Because that's all you'll get.

Here's the MO:

He knows more about the female orgasm than you do.

Although he's totally bald, there's a hairdryer and conditioner in his bathroom.

He's available either Friday *or* Saturday evening, never both, because his seventeen-year-old son "likes him home" on weekend nights. *Riiiiiight.*

You get your period at his place and he just happens to have tampons on hand.

He makes eye contact with you at a party, and his ring finger shoots straight into his pocket. It doesn't come out for the rest of the evening. Sketchy.

He doesn't post a photo on his Internet profile, and he can only be reached by cell phone.

He tells you he's going to a spa next weekend by himself. Straight men do not soak in rose-petal baths alone.

He can't see you on Friday night because he's going to the movies with a friend. Later he mentions that they saw a French film with subtitles. You can safely assume that the friend was not a guy.

He cancels plans at the last minute: he's sick; his son is sick; his son's dog is sick. When these get old, he scans the newspaper and pleads, "Can't make it tonight. The Dow Jones Industrial Average went down."

He's big on public displays of affection, except in his own neighborhood, where he walks three feet ahead of you.

Whenever you're at his place, his answering machine blinks with at least fifteen new messages, and he never plays them in your presence.

Neither of his ex-wives is on speaking terms with him, and one of them crosses the street every time she sees him. Even against traffic.

Since his divorce, he's sunk 100 percent of his disposable income into his bedroom and master bath, creating a hedonist's playground to rival Hef's grotto.

During an intimate moment, he reaches under his bed and pulls out a wicker basket brimming with vibrators. Take your pick. You notice that none are in their original wrappers. Did he wipe them down with alcohol swabs? Eeeeeeeew!

In the morning, he steams fresh cappuccinos, whips up mimosas, and flips a perfect omelet with one hand. After breakfast in bed, he turns on the shower and gets it "just so" for you. Then he lays out a shower cap, a women's terry robe, and perfumed soap.

He invites you to spend the afternoon at his pool. It is surrounded by a thicket of trees for maximum privacy. A bottle of Dom Perignon chills on the patio, and the outdoor sound system softly plays "The Girl from Ipanema."

While the two of you are sipping and skinny-dipping, your eye alights on a bikini top draped over a lounge chair. It has enormous cups. He nonchalantly explains that his neighbor uses the pool when he's not around. He's so smooth and sincere, and you're so looped on champagne, that you don't even think to ask how she managed to walk home topless.

Food for thought.

Hasta la vista, baby

After a few months of steady dating, you find out that last weekend he went clubbing in South Beach with a waitress he met at Hooters. X him out and move on. Which of the following is the most mature way?

A) Delete his e-mail address and cell phone number, and promise yourself never to use them again. Delete old e-mails, text messages, and saved voicemail from him. Delete *him.*

B) Settle in with some Häagen-Dazs and a *Sex and the City* DVD. Ask three single girlfriends to join you. Fuck guys.

C) Clean his junk out of your bathroom. Mail his nose-hair clipper and Pez dispenser full of Viagra back to him, along with an amiable note that says, "Thought you'd be needing these."

D) Draw pictures of his teeny-tiny penis, and make a

collage. Hang it on the wall and buy yourself a set of darts. Remember to protect the wall.

E) Invite him over, and when he falls asleep, paint **DOUCHEBAG** across his back in scarlet nail polish. Alternatively, you could Super Glue his buttocks together.[23]

Correct answers: A and B (easy on the mint chocolate chip). But C, D, and certainly E will work in a pinch.

General red flag dating

This category includes men who are not ready to have a relationship with anyone more warm-blooded than a pet iguana. Or they have manners so bad, you'd be embarrassed to bring them to White Castle. Unlike players, they won't go MIA on you. But you'll have to join the federal witness protection program to get rid of them.

[23] Source: "Man sues ex-girlfriend over glued genitals," http://crimeshots.com/forums/showthread.php?t=1659

Nip it in the bud if...

- He mentions on your first date that his psychiatrist thinks he's a narcissist. One so unusual and fascinating, she's upped him to thrice-weekly sessions. *Hel-lo?*
- He shares his profound wisdom: "If you can take care of a plant, you can be in a relationship."
- He explains why he left his wife: "She was in a coma. It was kind of a drag."
- He describes his two-year-old granddaughter as a dullard.
- He can't remember which of his three marriages produced his son. But what the heck, he's a great kid.
- Fifty percent of his conversation is peppered with "we," "us," and "our relationship." Meanwhile, you haven't even told him your last name.
- At the end of a pleasant evening, he politely requests a pair of your panties to add to his collection. Used.
- As if. Your thongs cost $20 a pair. New.

Prognosis: negative

In the middle of a heavy make-out session on the couch, he jumps up and announces, "I'm not ready." Possibilities:

    1) He's in another relationship.

    2) He can't get an erection.

    3) He's gay.

    4) All of the above.

He tells you that both his ex-wives, plus the three women he dated between marriages, all cheated on him. Does he mistrust women, or is he lousy in bed? And either way, does it really matter?

He shares custody of Smoochie, the yorkie-poo that he and his previous girlfriend adopted. They routinely call each other to confer about Smoochie's bowel movements.

You meet him through match.com and show his profile to your friend. What a coincidence! She dated him too, from the very same Internet site! Six years ago. Send him back to the recycling bin.

You ask him if his former wife of fifteen years had orgasms, because he can't seem to give you one. "I don't know," he muses. "I wasn't paying attention."

He's sorry he couldn't see you on Friday night. But how could he miss that Zen lecture on NOTHINGNESS? No-brainer.

As you're strolling together, he stops to buy a hot dog. Before you realize that he never offered you one, he's wiping the mustard off his lips. He's either incurably self-involved or has an eating disorder. Maybe both.

Call it quits if you've been dating for a year and...

- He has a conniption fit because you left your toothbrush in his bathroom.
- You declare that you're falling in love with him. The next day, he admits himself into the hospital with a heart arrhythmia.
- Every time you mention moving in together, he says he's not ready. Then he gets a rent increase, and suddenly feels emotionally prepared to take the leap.
- At his cousin's wedding, he introduces you to his relatives as "my co-worker, Ellen."
- He can't peel himself away from his job to take a vacation with you, even for a weekend. You finally offer to pay for an all-inclusive, five-day Caribbean cruise for two, and he's free as a bird.
- When you dock at St. Maarten at sunset, you ask him where he sees the relationship going. He shrugs and says, "You're there."

- Lately he's been asking, "Do you prefer platinum or gold?" However, once you sign your divorce decree, he suddenly has a lot of business obligations. Never mind jewelry, he won't even give you a ring on the phone.

And in retrospect, who even needs to ask? Platinum, obvi.

Hunk or geezer? Neither!

Geezer: Once you hit your forties or fifties, an older man can be seriously old. If his grandchildren are the same age as your kids and he drops the phrase "hip replacement," you'll be sharing the halibut and baked potato (dry) at the early-bird special. Then he'll load your pocketbook with extra rolls and margarine packets—because ya never know, ya know?

On the other hand, there are benefits to dining out at 5 p.m. For one thing, you'll have the secret satisfaction of being the only woman in the restaurant who's wearing a leopard-print thong. Plus you'll have plenty of time to get to bingo at the Shriner's Club. And don't forget the convenience of handicapped parking spaces!

Hunk: Sure, it's a rush to flirt with the tanned, shirtless roofer with the six-pack abs who plays drums for a garage band on the side. But do you really want to play beer pong with his friends? Followed by a little mailbox baseball? And afterward, be called a MILF[24] behind your back?

You're entitled to a little fun, but resist the urge to get wasted with his crew, pay his rent, treat him to a pair of custom-made leather pants, or bail him out when he's busted for possession. He's not your son, and besides, he's likely to dump you for a cute young thing in a tube top, no stretch marks. Unless you're Demi Moore.

Boyfriend as transitional object

Remember how you couldn't part with Blankie when you were a tot? Then you grew up and didn't need Blankie anymore. So it goes with your first post-marital romp. A red-hot love affair may be just what the doctor ordered. And it's more fun than going on antidepressants, which can cause weight gain. So have a blast, but don't get carried away. If one of these signs describes your current relationship, it isn't gonna last:

You're having sex with a twenty-seven-year-old grad student in the back seat of his Volkswagen. Well, you

[24] Mom I'd like to fuck

don't want to wake his roommate, do you?

You're panting over an off-the-boat Italian landscaper whose sultry eyes and sexy accent make your heart race. All the better that you can't understand a word he says.

Your new loverboy is turned on by the romantic notion that it's a five-hour drive for you to see each other. To him, phone sex is by far the best kind.

You hear yourself making all kinds of excuses when you discuss him with your friends: "It's not *his* fault that he cheated on his wife and last three girlfriends. His parents never set boundaries."

You're equally and seriously involved with two different men at the same time. Together, they just about satisfy all of your needs. Mostly.

You've been dating him for a year and still have no plans to introduce him to your kids, and you'd rather not find out what your friends think of him.

The two of you spend most of your time at the Route 4 Hourly Rate Motel, and come to think of it, you probably wouldn't recognize him in daylight. Do you even stop to wonder if they clean the sheets?

LET'S REVIEW:
WHAT YOU NOW KNOW

✓ The REAL reason he can't see you on Friday nights.

✓ That woman who answers his home phone? Not the cleaning lady.

✓ That black lace camisole you found in his bathroom? Not his mother's.

✓ Just another remnant from the forgetful topless neighbor.

✓ A guys' night out never includes a movie with the word *amour* in the title.

✓ You're dating a winner—of the Players Cup.

✓ So listen up when he tells you his last girlfriend pulled a gun on him.

✓ How to play darts without a dartboard.

✓ If he left behind an army of embittered exes, there's a reason. Him.

✓ Yet you thought you could change him. Don't feel bad—we did too.

✓ He picked up a redhead at the NOTHINGNESS lecture.

✓ Why Super Glue is more versatile than duct tape.

✓ Every guy has his hobby. But jeez, does it have to involve your undies?

✓ Dating a senior citizen = discounted movie tickets.

✓ Your first love after your divorce won't be your last, especially if he's twenty-five, tattooed, and steals cars for a living.

PHASE VIII:
Baggage Check

*Y*ou and any guy you meet will arrive hefting a fair amount of luggage. After all, both of you come with histories: dead-and-buried marriages, crazy ex-spouses, children with attitudes, and a string of dating disasters. Not to mention knock-down, drag-out divorce proceedings and half the assets you formerly had, if you're lucky.

You think you're ready to leave the past behind. But sometimes bygones will not be bygones. Beth is encumbered by a whackadoodle ex who checked himself into a loony bin after knocking up a hooker. Plus he feels free to show up at her house uninvited at 2 a.m. With an erection. The guy she was dating saw this as over-the-weight-limit baggage and fled in his pj's, never to be heard from again. Wimp.

On the other hand, your new boyfriend might be planning a two-week camping trip in a pup tent with his son, who insists that Mom be included. You find this unacceptable. Your man doesn't understand why. After all, you both agreed that your kids come first.

How much weight can we haul around without incurring a penalty? It's important to recognize the difference between a carry-on bag and a steamer trunk.

Carry-on

These bags might not slide under the seat in front of you, and they don't have wheels. At first glance, they seem cumbersome. But this is as light as it gets for travelers who've logged some mileage. You won't find anyone normal who's toting less.

Your son, who just graduated from college, comes home to live "temporarily" with you and your boyfriend. For some reason, it takes him a year to find a job, which doesn't really seem to worry him much. He spends all day on the couch, under a blanket with the a/c blasting, closely following the competitive eating circuit on TV and getting Doritos crumbs under the buttons of the remote control. Your boyfriend grudgingly accepts this. But remember: you'll have to do the same when his son comes to stay with you, along with his pet boa constrictor.

Your boyfriend is such a nice guy that when his children say, "Jump," he asks, "How high?" And you love him for it. So when his kids decide, on the spur of the moment, to crash your romantic getaway weekend, keep in mind that you're lucky to be included at all in the family's marathon game of Monopoly, even if the outdoor hot tub goes unused.

You just celebrated your boyfriend's daughter's wedding. You notice that among three hundred proofs, there are group shots of him, his ex-wife, the bride and groom, grandmas, grandpas, in-laws, and outlaws. Not to mention the maid of honor, best man, junior bridesmaids, and Father Flanagan. There's even a picture of your boyfriend shaking hands with the head waiter. You appear once, in a table shot, obscured by obese Uncle Morris.

You're locked in a passionate embrace with your new bf when your ex calls, demanding that you put his Lionel train collection in a box and leave it on the porch. Immediately. Hopefully, your guy will know better than to ask questions.

Steamer trunk

This excess bulk definitely won't fit in the overhead compartment. As a matter of fact, it could take up a whole moving van, and it will certainly crowd you right out of the relationship.

On your first date, you learn way more than you want to know about his former wife, "the bipolar bitch on wheels," including her shopping addiction, criminal relatives, and raging PMS. You utter a silent prayer that your ex isn't out there at this moment, kvetching to some stranger about your hot flashes.

His teenage daughter insists on tagging along on your second date, and he lets her choose her favorite restaurant, Pizza Hut. And why is she looking forward to spending her Saturday night on your date anyway?

He and his wife have been working on their divorce for the past six years. It's just "complicated."

Every time there's a hurricane warning, he hops on a plane to Florida to pull down her storm shutters. In her one-bedroom apartment.

The minute a doctor tells him there might be something wrong with his health, he runs to call his ex.

They still take family vacations together "because the children asked us to." Separate bedrooms at the hotel do not make it okay.

His son calls his cell while he's at the movies with you, and they actually chat during the film. You duck as other patrons pelt him with Raisinets. You even throw a few yourself.

Although he's been divorced for five years, he continues to refer to his ex as "my wife."

In fact, he lives in a garden apartment in her house, and when you call him, her nasal whine greets you on his answering machine.

They regularly haggle over who owes what for the kids' overdue library books.

His daughter texts him constantly, especially when he's out with you. In the middle of dinner, he abruptly plunks cash on the table and leaves you to get home by yourself, because she wants to be picked up at the mall. NOW.

He still attends weekly family therapy with his ex-wife and kids, and they all go out to dinner afterward.

He doesn't need a therapist. He needs a porter. Leave him and his Samsonite five-piece set at the carousel.

Help him unpack

Your boyfriend wakes up next to you and feels compelled to report that last night he dreamed he had sex with his ex-wife. What is the most constructive response?

A) Demand to know who was on top.

B) Next time he wants to fool around, tell him he can just smack the yak till it spits back.[25] (Note: this is not animal cruelty.)

C) Wait until he's feeling amorous, then announce that you had a sex dream about *your* ex. Wearing hand-cuffs and leather.

D) Point out that there are some dreams best not shared with anyone except the analyst he's been seeing three times a week for the past five years.

Correct answer: D, if you feel like making love; A, B, or C if you don't.

---

[25] Tug the slug; flog the frog; pump the python

Unclaimed luggage

Sometimes dusty baggage accumulates because a guy has lived alone for too long after his divorce. This can be really disgusting and often involves unsanitary conditions.

His idea of a long-term relationship is six weeks.

He sees nothing wrong with passing gas while you're standing next to him. In an elevator. Hey, it's natural.

He has to kick four jumbo laundry bags out of the way to open his apartment door.

You're overwhelmed by an odor when you walk in: eau de locker room.

His countertops are covered with sticky cereal bowls and half-empty cartons of beef lo mein. Not to mention a nasty fruit fly problem.

His stove is spotlessly clean and the instruction book is still inside the oven.

Ditto the dishwasher.

In his freezer, two-year-old Hungry Man dinners are embedded in glacial ice.

He orders a large anchovy and pineapple pizza, never asking what toppings you might like.

On his shelves, where normal people would keep books, he stores his extensive porn collection. It's alphabetized.

His living room furniture is comprised of the following items:

- PlayStation 3, Xbox 360, Nintendo Wii
- Prized collection of vintage video-game systems
- Stacks of Japanese comic books
- 52" flat-screen plasma TV
- Dolby surround sound speaker system
- State-of-the-art computer
- Half-eaten microwave burrito

There's no soap in his bathroom. God forbid a hand towel.

The mirror and walls are the same color: smudge.

The toilet seat is permanently up. In fact, he lost the cover years ago. Long story.

His bedroom walls are papered with magazine photo spreads of *Sports Illustrated* swimsuit models. What?! It's artistic!

You wonder why all of your dates end up at your place. He explains, "I like to keep my cave to myself." True story.

On a movie date, the two of you arrive fifteen minutes early. He chooses to wait in the car and clip his toenails. Later, you insist on separate popcorn.

Quite rightly.

LET'S REVIEW:
WHAT YOU NOW KNOW

✓ It's a tight fit to cram twenty-five years into a tote bag.

✓ Or three people into a pup tent.

✓ Boa constrictors prefer a diet of live rodents.

✓ Your boyfriend's ex-wife gets constipated before her period.

✓ You had to hear that over the Sausage Lover's pizza.

✓ While his fifteen-year-old daughter glowered at you.

✓ You're PNG[26] at your boyfriend's family galas.

✓ Lots of euphemisms for his *ménage à moi*.

✓ It's not healthy if he and his ex routinely call the cops on each other.

[26] Persona non grata

✓ Or discuss co-parenting issues in dimly lit restaurants.

✓ It's normal to have a sex dream about your ex.

✓ Which means he probably had one about you.

✓ Ick.

✓ Men who remain alone for too long collect boy toys.

✓ And turn into undomesticated animals.

✓ Plus they smell.

PHASE IX:
Moving On

$\mathcal{Y}$ ou're getting comfortable with your new life, but it's still two steps forward, one step back.

On the bad days, you're genuflecting on bended knee in the hope that your ex and his girlfriend will contract the bird flu, or at least come down with the clap. Praised be. No one else can read your thoughts, so this wish is really okay. You also have cheerier days, when you don't care which venereal disease they become riddled with. Or blinded and crippled from, and horribly disfigured too.

Then there are transcendent moments, like when you rip up that incendiary letter to your ex instead of mailing it. Which is a good thing, because it started with, "We both know that you're incapable of caring about anybody except yourself. However…"

The process of putting all this behind you is like being on a roller coaster when the amusement park attendant has gone for a long, long coffee break, and you're not sure if he's ever coming back.

During the wait, you scroll through the Infectious

Diseases Information Index[27] and let your mind wander—anywhere from flesh-eating bacteria to something only mildly itchy and dirty that they could pick up in a Jacuzzi. A tiny hungry parasite, for instance. See? You're inching forward. Read our checklists and find out how far you've come.

Bite your tongue

Remember your mother's age-old advice when you talk to the kids about Dad's shenanigans: "If you don't have anything nice to say, don't say it." We would add, "Lie through your teeth instead." Then give yourself a pat on the back for being a great mom.

> **You say:** "Daddy and Mommy both love you very much, but Daddy and Mommy have fallen out of love with each other."
> **You really mean**: *Your father is making a fool of himself with a 6'2" behemoth who's squeezed into an F-cup bra and speaks only Russian.*
> **You say:** "Dad is a little confused right now."
> **You really mean:** *Your father is a deeply disturbed putz.*[28]
> **You say:** "It will be fun for just you and me to move into a cozy apartment. You can even choose the paint color for your new room."

[27] cdc.gov
[28] Bozo with small prick

You really mean: *I'll be sleeping on a pullout in the living room—because your father spent a bundle on that McMansion with the mirrored bedroom ceiling and heart-shaped tub.*

You say: "Guess what! You're going to be the flower girl in Daddy's wedding."

You really mean: *And your new stepmother is the same age as your babysitter. In fact, she* was *your babysitter. Fun.*

You say: "Remind Dad that your tuition bill is due."

You really mean: *I hope he didn't drain your college fund on that chickenhead's[29] three-carat rock.*

You say: "How nice of Dad to line up that summer job for you."

You really mean: *It's just like that smarmy worm to try to score easy brownie points with you kids.*

You say: "I'm thrilled that Dad was able to get you tickets to that sold-out Dylan concert."

You really mean: *Of course he can throw around $300 to impress you. Meanwhile the bum didn't cough up a dime for your braces.*

You say: "How exciting! You're going to have a new baby sister or brother."

You really mean: *I can't wait to see the dark circles on your fifty-five-year-old father after he's been up all night with a puking infant.*

---

[29] A blowjob artist whose head is always seen bobbing back and forth in the manner of barnyard fowl

Do not pass GO, do not collect $200

On the days when your progress is stalled, you'll engage in some highly irrational behavior. Be honest with yourself. If three or more of these descriptions sound embarrassingly familiar, take a yoga class and start chanting "ommm." At the very least, you'll become flexible enough to zip up the back of your own dress, a crucial skill when you're single.

Still chopping up photos of your former hubby, you beg your computer technician to scan the severed heads into an S&M website. And send the link to your ex's boss, girlfriend, therapist, and mother.

You catch yourself flipping through the Yellow Pages, searching for "Hit Men."

Fortunately, you don't find any.

Although . . . until the divorce is final, he can't change his life insurance policy. And couldn't you just see yourself on a float in Tahiti, living off that fat half-million?

Maybe you should try searching again under "Problem Solvers."

You refuse to date Libras or Scorpios, because your ex was born on the cusp.

You're suspicious of any man who drives a sports car.

You call the guy you're dating and hang up, just to see

if he really is at home helping his son with his multiplication tables.

You've never been religious, but when you hear that your ex has an inflamed prostate, you're convinced there is a God, and She is just.

As far as you're concerned, the lowest life form, beneath rats, snakes, and weasels, is the subspecies known as ex-husbands.

Although you got a big raise and promotion at work, there's something missing. You're still festering over the news that your ex dieted off some excess lard.

Through stealthy Googling, you identify the woman he's dating and call her regularly at 3 a.m., breathing heavily into the phone and pretending that you're a stalker—which, by the way, you are.

You drive by her house, see his car parked in front, and are seized with an uncontrollable urge to slash his tires.

You settle for spray paint.

You run into your ex and his girlfriend at your son's track meet. Afterward, you badger the kid with questions like, "What?! Tell me she doesn't have some major junk in her trunk!"[30]

Every time he returns from seeing his father, you say the same thing: "I heard he gained a lot of weight. How did his chins look?"

[30] badonkadonk

Your computer freezes up and you break into a cold sweat, phoning your daughter at 8 a.m. on a Saturday for emergency assistance. She figures out that your wireless mouse just needs a couple of fresh batteries, and carefully instructs you to look for the + and − ends.

Whenever your son comes home to visit, you have a list for him: change the light bulbs; download the photos from your camera; reset the clocks to Daylight Savings Time.

Everywhere you look, you see couples: beer-bellied couples, Hari Krishna couples, toothless couples, deranged couples, and especially, happy couples. You're convinced that you'll be the only human for whom there is no mate, even though your friend Suzanne insists: "There's a seat for every ass."

You're going through a case of wine a month by yourself.

Your shrink no longer returns your calls.

Neither does your computer technician.

You haven't shaved your legs in six weeks. Okay fine, eight.

There are multiple copies of the Serenity Prayer[31] in your life. You carry one in your wallet, keep another on your nightstand, and refer constantly to the copy on your refrigerator door.

[31] "God grant me the serenity to accept the things I cannot change; Courage to change the things I can; And wisdom to know the difference. . ."

In your mind, your ex's tall, willowy girlfriend is clearly anorexic, and you tell everybody so.

You're up all night obsessing over whether or not her boobs are real.

You finally conclude that they're faux. Almost definitely.

And yet . . . could that really be her original nose?

You'll have to sleep on it.

Fuck it, you'll take a Valium.

Sticky situations

Unless your ex moved to an ashram in India, never to return to Western civilization, you're likely to encounter awkward moments like these. Think about how you would handle them. Remember, there is no single correct answer. Just find the one that says you.

1. At your daughter's graduation, you're standing amid a gaggle of relatives, yours and your ex's. Included in this intimate circle is his new wife, eight months pregnant. Nobody introduces you to her. These are your options:

A) Politely shake her hand while mumbling, "Eat shit and die."
B) Congratulate her and note that older fathers are more nurturing because their testosterone levels are shot.
C) Ask your former mother-in-law, at full volume, if this is the one she referred to as "that dumpy little bitch."
D) Muse aloud about breastfeeding vis-à-vis silicone leakage.
E) Pull your ex aside and snort, "Fast work. She seems like a nice kid."

2. Out of respect for your children, you attend your former father-in-law's funeral, even though your ex is bring-

ing the buttaface[32] he was seeing behind your back for two years. At a family gathering afterwards, she offers to pour you a drink. Here are your choices:

A) Give her a friendly handshake. "Hi Stacy, long time no see."
   "You know my name is Heather," she replies.
   "Terribly sorry," you say. "I just can't seem to keep you all straight."
B) Chat her up about the time your ex gave you a little chlamydia as an anniversary gift.
C) Sneak outside and key her car.
D) Ask her for a glass of red wine, and dump it over her head. Oops! So sorry! What a butterfingers.
E) Then offer her a tissue.

[32] Great body, but her face looks like the rear end of a baboon

Give yourself a gold star

The anger management seminar helped a lot. You're no longer preoccupied with murderous thoughts about your ex. And you don't come unhinged every time the toilet won't flush. You're making strides if you can take credit for even one of these class acts.

Feasting on caviar, blinis, and Stoli, you and your girl-friends hold a raucous toast to your ex's future. May his upcoming marriage, to his Russian fiancée Svetlana, last forever. His new soul mate knows exactly two words in English: "Tiffany's" and "bling."

Six months later, he begs you to take him back. You realize you're better off without him. He'll just have to find somebody else now that Svetlana maxed out his credit cards and hightailed it back to Odessa.

Since he got fleeced and dumped, you charitably pack a Thanksgiving box dinner for him and his mother. (Twenty-five bonus points for the microwave instructions.)

Your daughter has titled her college essay, "My Mother: I Think I'll Keep Her." A year ago she wrote a story called, "My Dad Left Me, My Mom, and My Dog for a Trailer-Trash Bimbo, and All I Got Was This Stupid T-Shirt."

You recognize that your worst nightmares about divorce didn't come true. You don't have to live at the Y with a communal bathroom down the hall, and you can still afford the granola at Whole Foods.

As a result, you've weaned yourself off Xanax.

And you no longer wake up screaming for fear that twenty-five years from now, your corpse will lie rotting in a tattered wedding gown, on a fold-up cot, in a squalid apartment, shrouded with cobwebs, for ten days, during which nobody has even called your voicemail.

You're now thinking five-year plan and are busy mapping out the boutiques on the rue Saint-Honoré in Paris. In fact, you've just perfected your *"Je t'aime,"* with properly pursed lips.

You realize that if anything happens to you, your ex will care for your children. You have evolved to the point where you're glad he's not dead.

Sometimes. Bravo all the same.

You finally concede that his girlfriend, the Restylane junkie, is attractive—if one goes for that "just plasticized" look.

You no longer fixate on her unibrow.

It's been weeks since you prayed for her implants to rupture. In a public place.

Or intimated to anyone that she's transgender.

He, on the other hand, looks like a beached whale with a weave.

Yet you say nothing.

You can now go out during *Desperate Housewives*. You finally figured out how to program your TiVo.

While scrutinizing the Weber Grill Owner's Guide, you (Step 1) disconnect the empty propane tank, (Step 2) get it refilled, and (Step 3) hook it up again—all without blowing up your house and car.

You're no longer despised by colleagues for being the office geek who fires off URGENT/HIGH PRIORITY e-mails at 11 p.m., just to avoid going home to an empty apartment.

You don't panic that you'll get lost every time you have to drive someplace unfamiliar. You've replaced your ex with an awesome GPS navigation system.

You remember him on his fiftieth birthday and send him a gift. No matter that it's a T-shirt with **OVER THE HILL** emblazoned across the chest.

On the card, you congratulate him for being one year closer to death than he is to birth. Thoughtful.

You devote an entire weekend to helping your daughter find an outfit for her father's vegan wedding to ***Traci, Spiritual Consultant & Tarot Card Reader***. This isn't easy, because neither of you knows the proper attire for a ceremony conducted by a shaman, at sunrise, in a positive energy field, in Taos. Without a prenup.

It's a very spiritual occasion, so you buy her a $500

dress. And have the bill sent directly to him.

Your ex sprints by, huffing and puffing behind the jogging baby stroller. "From a distance, you look really young," he says, gasping for breath. Though tempted, you do NOT do any of the following:

A) Shoot back: "From close up, *you* look like a grandpa."

B) Suggest that he's having a heart attack.

C) Observe that a college education in eighteen years is projected to cost $450,000. Joke that he'll be paying tuition with his Social Security checks.

D) Stick out your foot and trip him.

Don't you feel terrific about your self-restraint?[33]

You no longer believe that men are from another planet. You finally understand that they're just wired incorrectly. *Completely* incorrectly.

Your liquor bill has decreased by half.

Your shrink says you can cut back to one session a week. Provided you stop calling her at home.

You've scaled down to only a single copy of the Serenity Prayer in your home.

And once in a while, it even works.

---

[33] Okay, so you didn't have a snappy comeback at the time. Same thing.

PEACE PACT

No matter how far you've come, you still find your ex about as pleasant as a hemorrhoid flare-up. But you share the same kids, so like it or not you have to stay in touch. How can you do this without squabbling like a couple of six-year-olds?

Our friend Joanne and her ex, George, have come up with a system to avoid name-calling and childish quarrels: they communicate only through businesslike messages left on each other's cell phones. By constantly checking their caller IDs, they make sure they never have to converse. So when Joanne's phone rings and the words "Ugly Lardsack" pop up on her screen, she knows it's George and hits "Ignore." George does the same anytime "Fartface" flashes across his screen. *Voilà*. Maturity.

LET'S REVIEW:
WHAT YOU NOW KNOW

✓ A strategically bent coat hanger can be used to zip up your dress.

✓ Svetlana was no fool. *Nyet*.

✓ How to file an individual tax return.

✓ Never throw away any instruction manual.

✓ At the wedding, Traci wore a diamond nose ring, Birkenstocks, and a goddess sarong of ahimsa silk.[34]

✓ The groom wore hair plugs and a comfort stretch tux, size 44 Portly Short.

✓ His new bride isn't anorexic. In fact, she's in her third trimester, and waddling.

✓ Tissues do nothing for red wine stains. But you already knew that.

✓ It's perfectly normal to wish your ex would croak.

[34] Processed without injuring silkworms

- ✓ But it's enough to know that he's changing diapers at age fifty-nine.

- ✓ Still, it would be more cathartic to egg his car.

- ✓ A Subaru wagon with a BABY ON BOARD bumper sticker.

- ✓ His new wife is an über-boober.[35]

- ✓ Every word of the Serenity Prayer, by heart.

[35] Smug public breast-feeding fanatic, tutors at the La Leche League. Syn: lactivist.

PHASE X:
Happily Even After

Once upon a time you were desperate, searching Internet dating sites for men who had at least one feature in common with Johnny Depp. You lined up back-to-back Starbucks dates five nights a week, like a series of dead-end job interviews. Whenever something kindled, it quickly sputtered out. He didn't want an LTR[36] after all.

Then the pendulum swung the other way. That twenty-minute date—with the gasbag who yammered on about his son's 4.0 GPA—sealed the deal. You swore off men like a toxic drug habit, and half-joked about joining a lesbian mothers' commune. *Half.*

Now you're so busy that you don't even count, much less weep over, all those dateless weekends on your calendar. In fact, you'd rather stay home than go out with a guy who isn't even shampoo-worthy.[37] Without realizing it, you've learned how to enjoy an evening alone, searing

[36] Long-term relationship
[37] Worth washing your hair for

tuna for one rather than hunkering down over the usual bowl of Special K, slurped with a glass of merlot.

Think of every miserable date and half-baked relationship as your behavior modification therapy. You now avoid the guys who arrive at your door clutching a restaurant two-fer book. As well as those who profess their undying love—but only when they're on a different continent.

You can do better. You *know* you can. Are you ready? Get out there.

Charles and Camilla? NOT!

Who was the sadist who insisted that you have to kiss a hundred frogs before you meet your prince? *Puh-leeze.* We'd puckered up for maybe a dozen horny toads, and by the time we wiped the slime off our lips, we were downloading applications for a nunnery.

But the fact remains: after your husband dumps you for a bosomy Barbie doll, you need to hear, over and over again, that you're sexy and alluring, and most important, that some men prefer grapes to melons. You're drawn to charmers who have perfected the art of sweeping you off your feet. Let's see how grounded you are these days. Following are two personal ads. We hope that by now you know whom to choose.

BACHELOR NUMBER ONE

"Fit, successful Adonis, 46, looking to spoil the lady of my dreams with flowers and candlelit dinners. Love snuggling in front of the fireplace and sunset strolls on the beach. You are slim-pretty-cute. I am your white knight. Where have you been all my life?"

BACHELOR NUMBER TWO

"Hard-working, devoted single dad, hoping to get back into shape soon. Fond of bird-watching and Costco shopping sprees. In search of warm, intelligent woman who likes to do the Sunday crossword puzzle in ink."

If you picked Bachelor Number One, you're as superficial as we were. Let's deconstruct.

Fit = He's the meathead who's pumping his biceps at the gym—juiced up on steroids and grunting like a wild boar.

Successful = So how is he at the gym three hours a day?

Adonis = Narcissus.

Flowers/candlelit dinners = He plans to get you into bed pronto.

Sunsets, beaches, and you = He took a course on What Women Want to Hear 101.

Slim-pretty-cute = Check your brain at the door.

White knight = He wants a damsel in distress, because he doesn't feel like a MAN around a woman who can light her own gas grill.

Where have you been all my life? = He's been single for forty-six (probably fifty-six) years because no woman has ever been quite good enough.

You probably yawned right past Bachelor Number Two, unless you've been bamboozled by enough bullfrogs to recognize the difference. Let's see who he really is.

Hard-working = He doesn't spend half the week polishing his résumé, and the other half playing the slots at Mohegan Sun.

Devoted single dad = He coaches both his kids' baseball teams every weekend. He has no interest in playing the field.

Hoping to get back into shape = Who wants a guy whose belly is flatter than yours anyway?

Bird-watching/Costco = He's willing to expose the

nerdiest parts of himself and will embrace yours—
including your passion for pink porcelain poodles.

Seeking warm, intelligent woman = He's capable of
looking beyond your boobs.

Sunday puzzle in ink = Permanence doesn't scare
him. Plus he has a great vocabulary.

Ding Ding Ding! We have a winner.

Bye-bye BOB

*If Mr. Right sat next to you at open-school night, would you
even know enough to copy his e-mail address off the sign-in
sheet? Or do you still assume that all men are lying, cheating
scuzzbuckets, merely because your ex was catting around for
the last six years of your marriage?*

*Does this sound familiar? You have no weekend plans, so
you run through your cell phone directory, frantically searching for company. You stop breathing into a brown paper bag
only when you reach P, and your Pilates instructor agrees to
go to the movies with you. Your treat.*

*Or you break a date with your best friend because Gino,
your son's driver's ed instructor, invites you out for a spin in
the STUDENT DRIVER car.*

Chances are you'll keep making wrong turns until. . .

You're content to spend Saturday evening on a date with yourself. You order in Mu Shu Chicken, read any book that's not titled *What Men Want,* and slather your face with glorious green mud.

Now when you spend a Sunday at the art museum, you gaze at the Monets instead of the men. And you don't storm out, railing that all the handsome single guys are gay. Even though it's true.

You sign up for a group walking tour in Vermont, although hiking boots deeply offend your footwear aesthetics and you might have to pee in the woods.

You learn that the group consists only of couples and single women. You consider asking for a refund, fantasizing about a day at the spa instead. But when push comes to shove, off you go, with your Timberlands and a roll of toilet paper.

You've been busy. Between finishing the last six hundred pages of *War and Peace* for your book club and escorting seventy-pound Maybelle to doggie obedience class, you haven't even thought about going online to study before-and-after pics of Tara Reid's lumpy liposuction.

You spot a stray male squeezing honeydews in the produce section. The old you would have checked him out. The new you proceeds directly to the express line without so much as a glance at his ring finger.

You treat yourself to a chunky gold charm bracelet (after melting down the trinkets your ex gave you). You've even mastered the art of fastening it with one hand.

You'd much rather take a Thursday evening "Stitch'N Bitch" knitting class than face another endless night of bar hopping.

You realize that not every guy is Ted Bundy reincarnated. In fact, some of your best friends are men.

You finally feel comfortable dining solo at a trendy restaurant bar. You immerse yourself in *The Great Gatsby* while sipping a glass of pinot noir. You never even look over your shoulder to see if your ex is there with a busty blonde.

As a matter of fact, you no longer care what he and his young cupcake are up to, and whether hers are saline, silicone, or spectacular. (Totally silicone.)

A coworker tearfully confides that her husband went out for a pack of cigarettes and never came back. He's gaga for a tanorexic he met at the Tropicana Sun Salon. You know just what to tell her, because you heard it yourself from an A-list girlfriend, long, long ago:

"You're not going to believe me right now, but you WILL be happy again someday."

After work, you drive her straight to Victoria's Secret.

And refuse to let her leave without a jeweled g-string.

You assure her that washing instructions are beside the point.

Because this scanty strip of lace is an EMBLEM OF HOPE.

And she's not allowed to return it. Pinky swear.

Hello tomorrow

Fast-forward. Three years later.

Your ex bags his Wall Street job to study aura cleansing and holistic hair restoration. To his surprise, the firm does not reward his mind-body-spirit rebirth with a fat severance package. His new wife, Traci, shuffles the tarot deck and foresees canceled credit cards in her future. Uh-oh. Could this mean the end of her monthly "Heal Me/Pamper Me" spa retreats in Sedona? With a heavy heart, she immediately files for divorce.

Traci gamely picks herself up and achieves oneness with her Kabbalah instructor. They move to Oregon and open the Center for Re-enlightenment and Parapsychology (CRAP). With a tidy settlement from your ex.

He remains alone in the love nest, sleeping with his headboard facing east under a faceted crystal that dangles over the bed. True, Traci is no longer around to make his favorite dinner—fermented soybeans. But he *is* enjoying the positive chi flow. And really, what more could you ask?

Your kids are slightly embarrassed that their little half-sister's name is Rainbow Rabinowitz.

As for you . . . it turns out that the other lone diner at the bar was a Gatsby fan too, and divorced. His children actually seem to like you—a relief, because they used to refer to his last girlfriend, Agnes, as "Anus" behind her back.

The two of you have talked about moving in together. Your kids even concede that he's "okay," when pressed. But you're in no hurry. For the moment, you want to enjoy each other's company and see where it goes. The future is wide open, and that no longer makes you hyperventilate.

Because there are some things you do know for certain.

You can survive anything. You built a new life. You have fabulous underwear.

And who would have thought it? Someday came, and you're happy again.

Acknowledgments

We are indebted to Nina Schwartz, who expertly edited our work multiple times and always with perfect pitch; Will Schwartz, whose streetwise humor almost makes us seem cool; Paul Daly, who in addition to giving up a year's worth of weekends, read the manuscript at every stage and took us seriously even when it was ten pages long but we thought it was a book; and Shannon Whitaker-Burke, who added sharpness and style. Thanks also, for inspiration and funny contributions, to Debra Hershey, Midge Dell, Michelle Friedman, Jon Sirlin, Sonia Hendler, and of course, the many women who told all. Finally, we are grateful to Flip Brophy, Gerri Hirshey, and for her unflagging support, our agent, Marcy Posner.

About the Authors

Linda Reing began practicing for a career as a standup comic at age seven. When she realized this would mean performing in front of an audience, she changed gears, but has continued to embrace humor as her means of coping with the world. She lives in New York City.

Sue Mittenthal is a writer and editor whose work has appeared in *The New York Times, Esquire, New York Magazine, The Boston Globe, Glamour, Family Circle, Ladies' Home Journal, Readers Digest, Consumer Reports*, and other publications. She is currently a freelance writer in New York.

Sue and Linda met in a "Mommy and Me" music class with their toddlers in 1984. Some twenty years later they reconnected—both dumped, divorced, and dating. They have no idea how they found this humorous, but *Still Hot*, their first book, is the surprising and satisfying result.